SCH

Alan Henry is the Grand Prix Editor of the seminal weekly magazine, *Autocar*, and of the *Guardian* newspaper. He has covered Formula 1 since the early 1970s, which places him in a unique position among motoring writers as someone who has witnessed the development of Formula 1 in the modern age. A prolific author, his recent works include a biography of the 1996 World Champion, Damon Hill and a study of legendary Formula 1 drivers entitled *Racers*. The latter book was also published by Queensgate.

SCHUMI

ALAN HENRY

First published in 2000
by Queensgate Publications
Cookham, Berkshire

ISBN 1-902655-27-3

A catalogue record of this book is available from the British Library

Photographs by Formula 1 Pictures
Cover design by Charlie Webster
Book design by Production Line, Minster Lovell, Oxford
Production by Landmark Consultants, Princes Risborough, Buckinghamshire
Printed in England by Cox & Wyman

Contents

Introduction

The most expensive cap in the world

At just ten centimetres by eight, it is probably the smallest advertising logo carried by any professional sportsman anywhere in the world. Yet Michael Schumacher's cap is also probably the most expensive promotional billboard money can buy, after the German asset management company DVAG paid just over £5 million for it to carry its badging for the next three years.

Starting with the 2000 season, DVAG replaced Dekra, the German motor accessory chain, whose identification Schumacher had carried on his cap ever since winning his first World Championship driving for Benetton in 1994. This, of course, is in addition to the estimated £17 million annual retainer which Schumacher receives from Ferrari, for whom he is contracted to drive until the end of the 2002 season. The DVAG logo also adorned the shirts of German first division soccer club Kaiserlautern. But from the 2000 Australian Grand Prix it is set to compete for global television attention with the decals advertising Marlboro cigarettes, Shell fuel and oil, Bridgestone tyres and Federal Express which form the bulk of Ferrari's huge sponsorship portfolio, estimated to have paid Schumacher more than £65 million over the four seasons since he joined the famous Italian team at the start of 1996.

This enormous commercial influence says as much about the global status of Grand Prix racing as the sheer God-given ability of the young kid who cut his teeth racing karts on a local track close to his German home where his mother cooked hamburgers while he was flat out on opposite lock.

Michael Schumacher is not only recognized as possibly the greatest F1 driver of his generation; he is also one of the richest and most celebrated sportsmen in the world. One could reasonably add that Michael is also one of the most controversial drivers in the business, having been involved in more than his fair share of scrapes since making his F1 debut in 1991.

Moreover, with 35 Grand Prix wins to his credit by the end of the 1999 season, it is not too difficult to imagine Schumacher becoming the most successful F1 driver of all time by the time he eventually hangs up his helmet. Ahead of him remain only the records of the late Ayrton Senna (41 wins) and the all-time pace-setter Alain Prost on 51 victories.

Returning for a moment to Michael's commercial business, it is worth noting that Schumacher caps have long since assumed cult status among motorsport fans across the world. Approved facsimiles are assiduously marketed by Willi Weber, the astute Stuttgart-based entrepreneur who has managed both Michael and his brother Ralf from the very start of their motor racing careers. It is believed that the income from the sale of these Schumacher caps goes directly to Weber's management company as part of a deal he struck with Ferrari President Luca di Montezemolo when Michael signed to join the Italian team.

Unfortunately, Weber found himself accidentally tripped up by his own entrepreneurial flair at the 1998 Japanese Grand Prix when he organized a consignment of 'Michael Schumacher, World Champion 1998' caps to be delivered to the Suzuka circuit hotel. Unfortunately, in error, they were delivered on the eve of the race to the rival McLaren–Mercedes team official photographer.

The following day Schumacher failed to win the World Championship and these highly collectable caps were worn during Mika Häkkinen's title celebrations by a handful of Mercedes race personnel. With ironic relish!

Chapter One

Born to win

You are unlikely to find Michael Schumacher lolling comfortably in the adjacent seat to yourself on a scheduled air flight. The German multi-millionaire has long since passed the point where he needs to fly commercial – except for those gruelling long hauls to races in Australia, Japan and South America.

No, Schumacher is a member of F1 racing's five-star elite, with the wherewithal to bankroll his own exclusive travel arrangements. Not so long ago, Grand Prix drivers were just regular blokes, enjoying regular incomes and straightforward lifestyles. But it's not hard to understand why Schumacher, having enjoyed an annual income approaching $50 million for the past three years, finds his own executive jet just the job for convenience and privacy.

There is no doubt that Michael Schumacher is one of the very best Grand Prix drivers of his generation. A sporting technocrat; committed, focused and superbly fit. Yet his critics claim that he has earned himself a reputation as something of an enfant terrible in this most demanding and potentially hazardous of professional sports.

In the 1994 Australian Grand Prix at Adelaide, Schumacher's Benetton side-swiped British hero Damon Hill's Williams off the track and into retirement. This dubious manoeuvre meant that Michael, not Damon, won the World Championship. On that occasion Schumacher was given the benefit of the doubt. Yet when history seemingly repeated itself in the 1997 European Grand Prix at Jeréz and Schumacher's Ferrari rammed into Jacques Villeneuve's Williams, the episode certainly threw an unfortunate retrospective gloss on the collision in Australia three years earlier. This time his efforts at self-exculpation misfired and it was Villeneuve who survived to take the title crown. But Schumacher was unfazed.

'I certainly do not feel that my reputation has gone down after the collision at Jeréz,' he insisted afterwards. 'I believe that most people do not reduce the season to one race. Most make their assessment over the whole season. I am well aware that the 1997 season ended badly for me, but I have to look to the future.

'I have made a mistake and I cannot correct that wrong. All I want to do is to try and win the championship and repay the Ferrari team for the huge efforts they have expended in building the new car I will be driving.

'I think Ferrari definitely has the possibility to win this year's World Championship. Certainly, teams like McLaren and Williams will have made more progress, but we won five races last year with a car which was not as good as the one we have available to us this year.

'I would never say that I am the best. I'm not arrogant like that. Obviously Jacques Villeneuve won the World Championship, so he is the best at the moment. But it's up to us to prove that is wrong.'

For Ferrari, Schumacher's arrival has been akin to that of a Grand Prix Messiah. After years of struggling, the famous Team Maranello believed that this was the man who could lead them to the Promised Land. Three wins in his first season with them (1996), five in his second and six in his third suggested that this ambition was likely to be realized – eventually: for the 1999 season saw Michael crashing heavily on the opening lap of the British Grand Prix at Silverstone, effectively putting his hopes for a third Drivers' World Championship on hold until 2000 at the earliest.

Schumacher agrees that he has managed to bring a calming influence to the traditionally volatile Ferrari environment. 'I think I have been able to give consistency,' he said. 'In all teams, a driver has a certain responsibility to steer the team a little bit. Even if it is not too much, or too obvious, you can make the team nervous or keep it calm.

'I think in that respect I did the job in that I didn't become nervous at the time when it was difficult, when the other drivers would have become nervous and then, rather than improve, get even worse.'

Schumacher has always been a confident competitor. 'I remember well when somebody gave me the opportunity to test a Formula Ford car,' he laughs, 'and he said, "The guy is very quick in karting, but he will never be quick in a Formula car, because the driving style is so different." I think he was a little bit wrong there.'

The German has a boyish outward manner which conceals the sort of steely resolve and commitment which used to be associated with the late Ayrton Senna. However, if Schumacher lacks Senna's ascetic manner, projecting instead a freshly scrubbed image and more obvious outward enthusiasm, he has successfully laid claim to the Brazilian driver's crown at the very pinnacle of his chosen sport. Quite an achievement for a lad from modest surroundings who, little more than a decade ago, was scrambling round that little go-kart circuit in the German town of Kerpen, watched approvingly by his parents.

Senna, too, made himself a reputation as one of Grand Prix racing's Bad Lads. In 1988, on the opening lap of the Portuguese Grand Prix at Estoril, he tried to push his McLaren team-mate Alain Prost into the pit wall at around 180 mph. Prost later collared him and told him he hadn't appreciated that he wanted the World Championship so badly that he was prepared to die for it. Senna was briefly nonplussed, but two years later rammed Prost's Ferrari off the road on the first corner of the Japanese Grand Prix. It was a shameless move which settled the 1990 Championship in the Brazilian driver's favour.

Compared with all this wheel-banging drama, Grand Prix racing's bad boys in the past have been tame by comparison. Ferrari driver Lorenzo Bandini was mortified with embarrassment when a moment of over-exuberance saw him push Graham (father of Damon) Hill's BRM out of the 1964 World Championship contest at Mexico City. Graham later sent him a course of driving lessons for Christmas. Dry humour like that might be lost on many of today's top F1 stars.

James Hunt could be quite an aggressive performer, but he tended to keep his bad temper for when he was out of the car. At the 1977 Canadian Grand Prix he punched a trackside marshal, but the thought of pushing his friend Niki Lauda off the circuit as they battled for the World Championship would never have come remotely near his mind.

Today, however, Schumacher radiates the same sort of underlying confidence which so characterized Ayrton Senna:

an ingrained, taken-for-granted feeling that he is The Best. Yet there is none of the crackling volatility which lurked close to the surface of Senna's personality. In so many ways, Michael is the personification of Germanic cool. His sense of humour is kept under tight rein, yet he definitely has a more relaxed side to his character. Away from the pressure-cooker intensity of his racing, he will talk animatedly about his son and daughter, his dogs, and how much he and his wife Corinna enjoy the privacy of living in Switzerland.

But when the visor snaps down on the front of his racing helmet, Michael Schumacher takes on a very different persona. For him, Grand Prix racing is a matter for analytical concentration, not laughter.

Chapter Two

Through the ranks

So where did this young genius come from? Michael was born on 3 January 1969 at Hürth-Hermülhlheim, near Cologne, and was bought up in nearby Kerpen. His parents Rolf, a house-builder, and Elisabeth were not wealthy, but – like Mika Häkkinen's mother and father – they were prepared to back their sons in kart racing at the nearby track.

Michael admits that he was also extremely interested in football when he was a kid, an enthusiasm he retains to this day. Yet it was at the wheel of a kart that this shy and introspective teenager really came alive.

All who watched him in his early years agree that his talent came from sheer natural flair, a seat-of-the-pants ability. He had the sure, winning touch.

In 1984 Michael won the German junior kart championship, retaining his title the following year. In 1986 he was third in the senior championship, and then won that title again in 1987 together with the European crown.

Emboldened by his level of achievement, Michael graduated into the Formula Koenig single-seater category the following year and won the title while at the same time dovetailing this with a programme of European Formula Ford 1600 racing. In that latter category he finished second, some 30 points behind Mika Salo. Eleven seasons later the blond Finn would act as Michael's stand-in at Ferrari after the German ace broke his leg in the 1999 British Grand Prix.

In 1989, Weber recruited the young Michael Schumacher to drive for his own Formula Three team. The two men have never looked back since, together getting richer than their wildest dreams. Schumacher's third place in that year's German F3 Championship really put him on the map, and he followed it up by winning the Championship the following year. But it was on the international sports car stage that his talent seriously began to be advertised.

On the strength of Michael's performance in Formula Three, Weber was able to negotiate a deal for him to join the Mercedes-Benz sports car racing team, where he and his fellow rising stars Karl Wendlinger and Heinz-Harald Frentzen were shrewdly promoted as German's new generation of future racing aces. Mercedes-Benz had chosen to ease back on to the international racing stage through their links with the Swiss-based Sauber sports car team. In the mid-1980s Sauber began to use the lightweight Mercedes 5-litre V8 as an ideal powerplant for its Group C racing ambitions, and in 1989 the cars dropped the Sauber preface and officially became works Mercedes entries.

For the 1990 season it was decided that these three young German drivers –Schumacher, Wendlinger and Frentzen – would be alternated alongside veteran racer Jochen Mass at the wheel of the Mercedes sports cars. As *Autocourse* recorded in its seasonal review:

Wendlinger, Schumacher and Frentzen [who appeared only at Donington] did an outstanding job all year, benefiting from the thousands of miles of testing they were allowed over the winter. Each combined pace with economy and was not afraid to fight it out with either the crew of the number one car, or old hands like [Martin] Brundle and [Jan] Lammers [who drove the rival Jaguars]. And, against expectations, mistakes were few: Schumacher had a big practice off in the rain at the Ring, Frentzen spun in the race at Donington and Wendlinger picked up a puncture when he hit a slower car at Montreal, but otherwise they drove impeccably.

As for Michael's personal Mercedes record, he finished second in the 1990 sports car races at Dijon-Prenois and the Nürburgring and shared the winning car – and set the fastest lap – at Mexico City.

In 1991 Schumacher continued to drive for Mercedes, winning the Autopolis race in Japan at the end of the season driving the flat-12 engined C291 contender which had been such a challenging car to develop. He shared that victory with Wendlinger, who would go on to become a member of the Sauber F1 team two seasons later.

At the 1991 Belgian Grand Prix, Michael was invited to drive for the Jordan F1 team, then in its first season and making quite a mark as a newcomer on the World Championship scene. He would be paired alongside Andrea de Cesaris after regular team driver Bertrand Gachot had been jailed in London as the result of a traffic incident where he had used a CS gas canister in a dispute with a taxi driver.

Despite his sports car prowess, Schumacher had never driven a Formula One car before being invited into the Jordan camp. Inevitably, this meant that he was something of an unknown quantity; but he finished qualifying at Spa seventh fastest, not only ahead of de Cesaris but also in front of Benetton driver Nelson Piquet, making an outstanding impression on the F1 community at his first attempt.

Michael's first F1 race ended after only a single corner, when the Jordan's clutch packed up, but already the young German driver was hot property. One man for whom the Belgian race had merely been further confirmation of what he'd already expected was Benetton engineering boss Tom Walkinshaw. He'd seen Schumacher racing the Mercedes sports cars against his own Jaguars and suspected that he was something really out of the ordinary. Now he was certain. As, indeed, was Eddie Jordan.

'It was instantly clear that Michael was very special,' said Eddie. 'We tested him on the south circuit at Silverstone, which in those days was a fairly hair-raising place. Within a few laps he was braking 15 metres later for the kink before the pits than anybody else who had previously driven the car, and we were signalling him that he should come in, because we thought he was going too quickly too soon.

'But Michael knew what he was doing. Within five minutes we were convinced that he was pretty special.'

Ken Tyrrell, similarly, recognized the same sort of natural talent in Schumacher that he had seen in Jackie Stewart thirty years ago. 'It is that terrific ability to put in a fantastically quick first lap at the start of a race,' he said. 'Stewart was exactly the same, easily the best of his generation. Now it's Schumacher; but we all want to see Michael challenged, otherwise he could run away with all the championships.'

After only one race for Jordan in 1991, Michael switched to the Benetton team – in controversial circumstances. For several years thereafter, Jordan would argue that this was a major breach of contract which would have to be resolved in a courtroom. Eventually, however, the matter was settled amicably, away from the public gaze.

Chapter Three

Benetton's million-dollar baby

The fortnight separating the 1991 Belgian and Italian Grands Prix saw frantic negotiations to get Schumacher out of his Jordan contract and into a Benetton. The result would see the 22-year-old German driver set up for a $4 million driving fee during his first full season with the team owned by the famous Italian knitwear dynasty.

With Bernie Ecclestone taking a hand in the contractual comings and goings, the deal was eventually done, leaving Jordan temporarily humiliated and vowing legal retribution. Much of the talking was carried out in that millionaire's playground and traditional home of the Grand Prix glitterati, the Villa d'Este hotel, which fronts on to Lake Como about 25 miles north of Monza.

Those present recall that Michael almost felt that the negotiations were spiralling beyond his control. Eddie Jordan believed that he had a firm contract with Schumacher. After the Belgian race Willi Weber and Mercedes competition chief Jochen Neerpasch had arrived in England to meet with Jordan in what seemed from the touchlines to be an attempt to amend the terms of the deal. Jordan, however, shied away.

Simultaneously, Neerpasch had also surprised Benetton's Tom Walkinshaw by asking whether he would be interested in Schumacher. Walkinshaw was initially surprised, understanding that Michael was already committed to Jordan. Soon afterwards came a fax from Neerpasch confirming that talks with Eddie had fallen through.

Jordan's objections notwithstanding, Michael duly arrived at the Benetton factory, where he had a seat fitting for the B191, and replaced Roberto Moreno in the Benetton squad. The German youngster now found himself lining up at Monza alongside the veteran Nelson Piquet, who was embarking on his 200th Grand Prix. Many people were inclined to the view that Piquet was now past his best; but, while the veteran Brazilian could perhaps no longer demonstrate the sort of form which had carried him to his three World Championship titles, his huge experience would prove enormously helpful to Schumacher.

At Monza, Michael started as he meant to go on, outrunning Piquet all weekend to finish fifth in the race, just over 10 seconds ahead of the Brazilian. The rest of the 1991 season went quite smoothly for Schumacher: he finished sixth in Portugal and Spain, but retired with a couple of mechanical failures and a collision in the other three races of the season. It was perhaps not the way he would have liked to end his first series of outings for the new team; but he had impressed the Benetton team enough already, and he continued to drive for them during 1992 and 1993.

Meanwhile, the hapless Moreno switched briefly to take Schumacher's place in the Jordan team for the Italian Grand Prix, but was then replaced by the promising young Alex Zanardi for the remaining races of the season.

The whole experience had been an unpleasant and somewhat stark lesson on the realities of Formula One politics for Eddie Jordan, who to this day believes that his team was extremely hard done by as a result of those negotiations in the summer of 1991.

In 1992 Michael finished several races in the top six, gaining more and more points in the Drivers' Championship. Then, in Belgium, exactly one year after his spectacular debut at the wheel of a Jordan, he took his maiden victory in treacherously wet/dry conditions, winning by nearly 40 seconds from Nigel Mansell's Williams–Renault.

It was a magnificent, well-judged performance from the young German ace, and many found it refreshing to see a driver actually enjoying himself on the podium after winning a race, jumping around all over the place with a huge smile on his face. This exuberance in victory would remain a quality of the German throughout his career.

The autumn of 1992 had also seen Benetton raise its game, moving from its rather confined headquarters at Witney, Oxfordshire, to a new 17-acre, 85,000 square foot factory a few miles away at Enstone, bringing a hitherto rather fragmented operation under a single roof. Engineering Director Tom Walkinshaw and Technical Director Ross Brawn quickly had the new headquarters well organized and it began to seem as though Benetton was approaching a position where it could challenge Williams consistently for a place at the front of the Formula One field.

Meanwhile, Schumacher ended his first full F1 season with 53 points, and nearly a second victory in Adelaide, when he ran closely behind the winner Gerhard Berger for the whole of the last 30 laps. However, in the event he would not win another Grand Prix until September 1993 in Estoril, where he beat Alain Prost and Damon Hill to the flag. He finished fourth in the championship that year, but his best seasons in Formula One were still yet to come. The next year, 1994, would prove to be the turning point in Schumacher's career.

Schumacher's team-mate in 1992 was the British driver Martin Brundle, who drove impressively throughout much of a crucial year during which he was measured against Michael's undoubted prowess. Brundle drove a blinding race to finish third in the British Grand Prix at Silverstone and also gave Michael something to think about when he dodged past him to take the lead in the Canadian Grand Prix at Montreal as they lapped a couple of slower cars. Only a driveshaft failure late in that race stood between Brundle and his first Grand Prix win.

'We were together in 1992 at Benetton and there was no doubt from the outset that Michael was incredibly quick, motivated and highly confident for one so young,' said Martin. 'He had such enormous faith in his own ability, but on the other hand, it came as a big shock to him when I blew him off in the British Grand Prix at Silverstone. I think he regarded me in a new light and had greater respect for me after that race. But there was no doubt, even then, that Michael was something special.

'In a debrief, he would press a point with engineers who had been in the game for years, even if he was wrong. I had never seen that before with someone so young.'

The 1994 season was the start of Schumacher's third full year with the Benetton team, and as yet there he had not had a huge amount of success, considering how well he had performed on his debut. However, the Benetton B194 chassis – powered by the compact and lightweight Ford HB V8 engine – had a claim to be the best car the team had produced, and combining this with the fact that their main rival's car, the Williams FW16, was not as good as the Williams team had hoped, things looked good for Schumacher and Benetton.

Indeed, at the first race of the season, in Brazil, Schumacher outdrove Ayrton Senna in the Williams; in his struggle to keep up with Schumacher, Senna spun near the end of the race and stalled his engine. Schumacher repeated this victory in the inaugural Pacific Grand Prix at Japan's lavish new TI Aida track, giving him a total of 20 points after only two races, while Senna had yet to score.

Ayrton found that the new Williams FW16 was difficult to drive on the limit, but major changes were made to it in time for the San Marino Grand Prix – where, the Brazilian confidently predicted things would be different.

'The World Championship starts at Imola,' said Senna. Tragically, for him it ended there. The Williams crashed while leading the race and the brilliant Brazilian driver died from his injuries. Michael went on to win at the end of a day when most of the F1 paddock wished it could have been anywhere else but at a motor race. The torch had passed.

Senna's death was certainly a deeply bruising episode for the entire F1 community, which closed ranks to protect itself from criticism from the outside world. Senna had been the sport's leader and, to a large extent, motor racing's senior category was now rudderless, without a man to set the pace and standards. Yet Michael Schumacher would quickly step forward to lay claim to Senna's fallen crown.

From that moment onwards, Schumacher began a run of domination, only to be dramatically frustrated by more aggravation, this time stemming from the British Grand Prix. On the final parade lap, Schumacher breached the rules by overtaking Damon Hill's Williams. The German driver was eventually shown a pit board indicating that he was due a stop–go penalty for this transgression, but enraged the governing body by staying out on the circuit while Flavio Briatore and Tom Walkinshaw, argued at length with the stewards. Eventually, Michael was black-flagged from the race and lost the six championship points for his second place. He was also given a two-race ban, but the team lodged an appeal which at least allowed him to race at Hockenheim in the German Grand Prix a fortnight later. On appeal, however, Benetton's fine was increased from $25,000 to $500,000 for their failure to obey the instructions of race officials.

Hockenheim heralded a further setback for Benetton with the team's second driver Jos Verstappen lucky to escape all but uninjured after a refuelling conflagration during a routine pit stop. Schumacher himself retired with engine problems, allowing Berger's Ferrari an easy win, but bounced back in Hungary, beating Hill's Williams with an audacious three-stop strategy to the Englishman's two stops.

Benetton was fortunate to escape from the Hockenheim fuel fire without an additional penalty. The fuel rig used for Verstappen's car had a filter missing, illegally speeding up its flow rate; but there were some ambiguities in the case which prevented the team from incurring further sanctions. As for Michael, his two-race suspension was upheld and he duly missed the Italian and Portuguese races – as well as incurring a disqualification in Belgium after excessive wear was detected in the B194's under-car skid block when it was checked after the race.

There was certainly an arrogance about Michael's behaviour during that 1994 season, maybe prompted by the inexperienced enthusiasm of youth, maybe just natural overconfidence. This mood certainly seemed to be encouraged by the Benetton squad, which also came under technical scrutiny from the sport's governing body when suspicions were aroused that the B194 was equipped with a system of traction control, illegal under that year's revised regulations.

A detailed examination of the Benetton's electronic software systems revealed that the B194 did indeed have an unmarked 'option 13' hidden within its system which provided a launch control to minimize wheelspin at the start of races. Michael had certainly produced some consistently spectacular starts throughout the '94 season, most notably at the French Grand Prix at Magny-Cours, where he darted through from third place on the grid to get ahead of the Williams FW16s of Damon Hill and Nigel Mansell by the time they reached the first corner.

The FIA technical delegate carried out a detailed investigation into the Benetton's systems and decided that 'the best evidence' was that they had not been used. Nevertheless, the whole episode cast an unfortunate light over the whole ethos of the team, creating an atmosphere of suspicion among its key rivals which inevitably lingered for some time.

Schumacher's disqualification at Spa, added to his absence from Monza and Estoril enabled Damon Hill to win all three of those races, vaulting into contention for the Championship, although in reality this was a somewhat artificial situation in that, adding the Silverstone disqualification to these later setbacks, Schumacher and Benetton between them had cost the German driver the chance of winning another 40 championship points from four races.

Michael returned to the fray at Jeréz, where he won the European Grand Prix – only to be beaten into second place by Hill in the rain-soaked Japanese Grand Prix at Suzuka. He then rounded off the season by clinching the 1994 World Championship by a single point in acutely controversial circumstances after colliding with Hill while battling for the lead of the Australian Grand Prix at Adelaide.

Whether Schumacher made an innocent error, or took a pragmatic decision to remove Hill from contention after he himself had inflicted potentially terminal damage to his Benetton by side-swiping a wall, has never been satisfactorily resolved. Suffice it to say that the 1994 season was one which the F1 fraternity was happy to put behind it.

For a while at Adelaide, it had looked as though Schumacher was feeling the pressure. He crashed heavily in Friday practice, eventually qualifying second behind Nigel Mansell, the 1992 World Champion who had returned from his interlude racing Indycars in North America to fill the role of Williams guest driver in the wake of Ayrton Senna's death. Damon Hill finished the first session third fastest, and this was his eventual place on the starting grid as Saturday's second qualifying session took place on a wet circuit.

The build-up on race-day morning understandably crackled with high-tension anticipation. Williams team insiders were privately worried that Hill hadn't managed to bag a place on the front row, but at least Damon knew that Mansell would help his Championship challenge. Nigel had pledged to get out of the way and let the two title protagonists get on with it.

Schumacher, for one, wasn't about to take Hill for granted. On the starting grid, the Benetton team leader gambled by reducing his car's aerodynamic downforce in the interests of straight line speed. It was a decision which would come within a few yards of costing him the World Championship.

The eyes of the world fell upon the starting grid as Mansell led the cars round the final parade lap. Red lights, green light – and suddenly they were away in an ear-splitting crash of sound, Schumacher's Benetton already pulling level with Mansell's pole-sitting Williams as they jostled into the tight chicane only a few hundred yards away from the grid. Nigel took a quick glance in his mirrors and cleared out of the way for Damon, moving over to the far right of the circuit to allow the other Williams FW16 through in its pursuit of the Benetton. By the end of the opening lap, Schumacher was a stupendous 2.1 seconds ahead of Hill, but that was as good as it got.

Both Michael and Damon were running on the same three-stop refuelling strategy and, by the end of the second lap, Hill had pulled back to only 0.4 seconds behind the leading Benetton. Nor was he hanging on by the skin of his teeth; he was seriously challenging Schumacher for first place.

For Michael, the penny suddenly dropped that he had a fight on his hands. The two leading cars were totally embroiled in their own private battle, blowing the opposition away like never before. Damon was soon lapping within a few tenths of his own third-place qualifying lap and, with only ten of the race's 81 laps completed, had opened an 18 second gap over Mika Häkkinen's McLaren–Peugeot in third.

At the end of lap 18 the atmosphere in the pit lane was absolutely electrifying as Michael and Damon came in for the first refuelling stops. Schumacher remained ahead as they accelerated back into the fray, but there were increasing signs that Hill was getting the upper hand when it came to slicing through the slower traffic. Then suddenly, mid-way round lap 36, the German ace made what looked like a crucial error.

Coming out of a medium-speed left-hander, the Benetton slid wide and glanced the concrete retaining wall. Crucially, Damon didn't witness this event: he had dropped back a few lengths and was out of sight of his rival round the previous corner. All he saw was Michael coming back on to the grass.

'I thought, "Hello, you've slipped up there,"' reflected Hill afterwards. 'But I thought his car was OK. Only when I later looked at the video was it clear that his right-rear suspension was pretty damaged and would have put him out of the race.

'Of course, it's easy if you want to look back in time. In retrospect, I would have let him go.'

For the next five seconds, the outcome of the 1994 World Championship was balanced on a knife-edge. As Schumacher was apparently recovering, Damon saw his chance and dived for the inside going into the next right-hander. Michael pulled across him, and the Benetton vaulted up on to two wheels as it rode over the Williams's left front corner, slammed back down on to the track and slid straight into the tyre barrier on the outside of the turn. Schumacher was out.

Hoping against hope that his Williams could be repaired, Damon limped back to the pits. But there was nothing to be done. The left front top wishbone on the FW16 had been bent beyond repair. Hill sat glowering in the cockpit for several minutes, absorbing the disappointment, then climbed out and strode into the Williams team office.

Almost as a footnote, Nigel Mansell won the race in the other Williams–Renault, but it was not a success calculated to secure his full-time return to the team in 1995. David Coulthard was eventually confirmed in that role.

It fell to Patrick Head to sum up on Hill's efforts in Adelaide.

'It was absolutely Damon's finest race,' he said firmly. 'He was a man on a mission and, had it not been for the accident, I have no doubts that he would have got the job done.'

Hill flew back to London in the role of gracious loser. The FIA examined all the available evidence surrounding the collision and decided there were no grounds for further action.

Damon remained dignified and aloof when it came to discussing the episode with Schumacher. The two men had met by chance in the breakfast room at their Adelaide hotel on the morning after the fateful race. Observers report that there was a slightly strained, yet good-mannered mood between them. If anything, said the outsider, Schumacher looked slightly uneasy.

'Damon came over and congratulated me and we talked it over,' said Michael. 'I did not get the feeling he was bitter about it.' Perhaps Schumacher was indulging in a moment of wishful thinking. Damon certainly had his own thoughts on the matter, but they were just that. His own. He was not inclined to share them with anybody else.

Yet Michael's assessment of the season as a whole, and that race in particular, was certainly measured. It betrayed no trace of self-doubt. By then Adelaide was history. Schumacher did, however, make some self-conscious observations which amounted to back-tracking over his previous remarks which had called Hill's talent into question.

'It was a great battle between me and Damon at the start of the race and I have to say he has done a really good job during it,' he admitted.

'We both didn't make mistakes and it was really, I would say, thrilling for you on the outside. I have to say I did make some comments this year about Damon that I didn't have the kind of respect for him that maybe I had for somebody else, but I have to admit that I was wrong.

'What he has done in the last two races in particular – and what he did before – has been a fantastic job. He has been a great rival and I must say sorry for what I maybe said. I'd like to congratulate him.

'Nevertheless, the feeling about the Championship. I nearly won it earlier this year and then I got banned for a couple of races and could not continue. I lost a lot of points, so I thought now it's going to be very, very tough and difficult to make this Championship up again. Just sitting here now having won it, it's a dream. I really can't explain what it means.

'To me it was always clear that I was not going to win the Championship, and that it was Ayrton who was. But he hasn't been here for the last races and I'd like to take this Championship and give it to him.

'He was the best driver, he had the best car and those are my feelings about him. It was difficult at the time to show those feelings to the outside world, but I always thought about it and it's the right time to do something about it, to give something I achieve – and he should have achieved – to him.'

For the 1995 season Benetton changed from Ford to Renault power, becoming the French engine supplier's second works-supported team alongside Williams. This looked quite logical at first glance; but there were considerable logistical and technical considerations to be taken into account, as Ross Brawn later reflected.

'We underestimated the problems involved, partly because we had not changed engine supplier for so long,' he said. 'Our 1994 car had been a good one because we had been together as a group at Benetton for three years, plus a much longer period with Cosworth. We had a nice package all round. Renault would prove to be fantastic and it was no disrespect to them when I say that any such transition was bound to be difficult.

'Things didn't quite work out as we'd hoped at first. At the beginning of the season we had a problem with the hydraulic pump drivers and there was also a problem with gearbox casings cracking due to vibrational stress. That really set us back quite a bit and we spent the first few races finding out feet. Williams had the advantage to start with.'

In fact, Schumacher opened the season with a victory in the Brazilian Grand Prix at Interlagos, his Benetton B195 heading home David Coulthard's similarly powered Williams FW17. However, even before the race it had been found that a fuel sample from both these cars did not match that which had previously been lodged with the FIA. Both Schumacher and Coulthard thus went to the starting grid knowing they were in trouble; but after an initial disqualification, both drivers were permitted to keep their Championship points, although the constructors were not.

Hill went on to win both the Argentine and San Marino Grands Prix where, respectively, Schumacher had a third place and an accident while leading. At the Imola race Schumacher was also admonished by FIA President Max Mosley for trying to circumvent the new rules which required that the all-up weight of a driver and car should be 595 kg from the start of the season. With cars now being weighed after the race with the driver not strapped into the cockpit, a heavier 'officially registered' driver weight would have offered potential for running the car itself lighter during the actual race. Schumacher tipped the scales at 77 kg during the official weigh-in – only to show up at 71.5 kg after the Brazilian Grand Prix!

'I think it is very unfortunate if a World Champion gets involved in a misunderstanding over how much he may or may not weigh at any time in a weekend,' said Mosley sternly. 'It reflects very poorly on the sport and shows a lack of an adult attitude towards it.'

After this disappointing start, Schumacher quickly got to grips with his Benetton B195, winning in Spain, Monaco and France before being elbowed off the road at Silverstone as Damon Hill tried an over-ambitious overtaking move in the British Grand Prix.

'What can I say?' shrugged Schumacher. 'I think what Damon did was totally unnecessary. In fact, it was totally stupid. There was no room for two cars and there is no place to overtake there.

'It is such a small straight and even if you brake in the first part, and you turn in, it's almost impossible, and I think if I hadn't been there he would have gone straight on and into the gravel. So he had absolutely no reason to attempt such an overtaking manoeuvre at that time.'

Schumacher's misfortune handed the initiative to his number two driver Johnny Herbert, who came through to post his first Grand Prix victory. He would do precisely the same at Monza after Damon and Michael again tangled during the Italian Grand Prix. On this occasion paddock opinion was pretty evenly divided over whether Damon had just blundered into a driving error or Michael had deliberately 'suckered' him into making an ill-judged passing bid.

The incident occurred at the second chicane. Michael and Damon were running in second and third places, the Benetton and Williams coming up to lap the Japanese driver Taki Inoue's Arrows as they rounded the fast Curva Grande right-hander which immediately precedes that chicane. In an effort to be helpful to the faster cars, Inoue hugged the inside line, which forced Schumacher and Hill to run round the outside of his car on the approach to the braking area for the chicane. Perhaps unsighted momentarily by Inoue – and anxious not to be split off from Schumacher – Hill left his braking extremely late and suddenly found himself plunging into the back of Michael's car as they arrived at the corner in question.

The two cars went spearing off into the gravel trap, ending the World Championship battle for another afternoon. Schumacher erupted from his Benetton's cockpit and looked set to give Hill a very abrupt piece of his mind before marshals tactfully steered him away from the Williams driver.

'I turned into the corner not expecting anything, just a normal entry into the corner,' fumed Michael. 'I was really late into the corner and was braking late compared to Gerhard and the other drivers. Suddenly I felt a big bang and Damon went into me.

'It was not a slight touch – he really crashed into me. I am certainly very upset about it, because it's the second time now and he's taken more points away from me which I could have gained by finishing in front of him.'

For his part, Hill was defensively apologetic. 'There wasn't much conversation,' he admitted. 'Obviously Michael is very upset, but I'm upset too. I wanted to have a really good race to the end, but when you've got people out there who are really clueless as to what's going on around them [a reference to the Arrows driver], then these things happen.

'I will never want to tangle deliberately or have an accident like that because it just ruins the race. Every time Michael got a bit of space, I managed to pull him back.'

Although Herbert won the race to score his second win of the season, it had been an uphill struggle for the popular English driver. 'I just can't drive the car the way Michael likes it set up,' he admitted. 'He has the car [set up] very twitchy and you need a lot of confidence to drive it like that on the limit.

'Quite honestly, it was an unfortunate time for Johnny to have joined the team,' admitted Ross Brawn. 'I believe that if he had been with us in 1994, he would have had a much happier season. The fact was that the car was not as good as we would have liked and, when faced with those circumstances, it's difficult to be fair about the responses you have to make to try and sort out the car.

'Given the situation we were in, I think it was proper that we used Michael to try and solve the problems as quickly as possible. He had been driving for us for four years, he was the quicker driver and certainly the one with the most experience.

'In fairness to Johnny, the comments he made about the car were correct. It's not that we didn't believe him; we were simply unable to address the things which troubled Johnny as quickly as we should have done, because those problems in some ways did not trouble Michael.

'Confidence level in the car was never a problem for Michael, which meant there were other things that we could get on with sorting out. Giving Johnny confidence in the car was not always our highest priority.

'I won't pretend that we did a fantastic job for Johnny, but we did the right job for the team under the circumstances we were faced with. As a result, we had a good crack at both Championships and Johnny won two races. There is a lot in Johnny but we were not in a position to get the most out of him. Under the circumstances, he deserved a lot more credit than perhaps he got for what he did achieve with Benetton in 1995.'

Meanwhile, Schumacher won nine races in total and helped Benetton clinch its first Constructors' Championship crown. The previous year Benetton and Williams had shared the honours, the drivers' crown going to Michael and the constructors' laurels to Williams. This time, however, Benetton marshalled all the efforts at its disposal to clinch both championships in decisive fashion.

However, for Benetton it was also the end of an era. The Schumacher era. For 1996 Michael would be moving to Ferrari as part of a reputed $25 million deal. The Italian fans were waiting with fevered anticipation. Schumacher would not let them down.

Chapter Four

Ferrari saviour

What made Michael so good? A pretty convincing explanation came from McLaren team chief Ron Dennis at the end of the 1995 season. It was a judgement which obviously carried a huge amount of weight because it was made by one of the most experienced and dispassionate F1 team principals in the business.

'Something I hardly ever get a chance to do is to see these guys out on the circuit actually driving,' he said after watching from the pits during practice for the second Pacific Grand Prix, the penultimate round of the 1995 title contest.

'But if you watched Schumacher in Aida you knew exactly why he was going to be on the front row and why he would win the race. He was mind-blowing. He just changes his style to suit the nature of the circuit – as Ayrton did – to such an extent.

'If it requires a track to be driven clean, he will drive it clean. If it requires the car to be thrown in and put sideways to scrub off speed as opposed to hitting the brakes and destabilizing it, that is what he will do.

'Monaco, for instance, has to be driven as if you are in a kart, but it takes so much car control. You have to get close to the barriers and use all the road.'

It was difficult to know quite what to expect of Schumacher at Ferrari. His early predictions that he was unlikely to score a World Championship hat trick in 1996 were shown to be a tactically conservative assessment of his prospects when he posted fourth fastest time at the wheel of his new Ferrari F310 during pre-practice testing for the Australian Grand Prix, the opening race on the F1 calendar and the first such event to take place on Melbourne's Albert Park circuit.

Demonstrating the long-term potential of the new Italian machine, Schumacher's best time was beaten only by the powerful Renault V10-engined Williams FW18s of Jacques Villeneuve and Damon Hill, plus the similarly powered Benetton B196 of Jean Alesi.

'I don't think we can fight for pole position,' said Schumacher. 'I expect that Williams and Hill are the best prepared to fight for pole position or victory right now, so I think it will not be a big challenge between the two of us this season.'

In the event, Michael failed to finish that first race of the year, retiring due to brake problems, while his newly recruited team-mate Eddie Irvine finished third behind Hill and Villeneuve.

The new Ferrari F310 had been the handiwork very largely of respected British engineer John Barnard, a man who had worked with pretty well most of the top Grand Prix aces of the previous decade and a half. He quickly recognized that Michael was another member of that elite group.

'People like Schumacher are a step up, on another level,' he said firmly. 'There are good guys out there, like Alesi and Berger. But then you have the special ones – Senna, Prost, I suppose Lauda, and, going back, the likes of Clark and Stewart.

'They are just bloody quick. There is no major philosophy about it. Michael also has a great deal of inbuilt confidence. He can produce very quick times and is obviously driving at that speed without any strain, without thinking about going quickly, because when he comes back he has a load of information in his head about all the corners around the track.

'In terms of how he likes the car handling, he wants the nose to turn into the corners at any time and he's prepared to dial the back end in and out – a high-wire act – by working the throttle.'

However, while Barnard admired Schumacher professionally, his long experience in the F1 business instinctively recognized a driver with a high opinion of his own talent. That made him hard to get to know.

'On a personal level, I find him difficult to warm to, or to get close to,' said John. 'It is hard to develop a close working relationship with him. He is also rather aloof, and certainly doesn't have any shortage of self-esteem. In some ways, I suspect that is because he is surrounded by a group of fawning acolytes who keep telling him how wonderful he is.

'On the other hand, the pressure on a young guy of that age must be enormous. All those millions of dollars, private jets and people falling over themselves to make a fuss of you. It's no wonder their heads get turned.'

The 1996 Championship battle turned into a close tussle for Hill, who only took the title by winning the very last race of the season in Japan. Yet as the year wore on, it became increasingly clear that Jacques Villeneuve was emerging as one of the great new talents on the F1 horizon. Thus it was almost pre-ordained that he should eventually find himself pitched into a head-to-head confrontation with Michael

Schumacher, the driver regarded as the most gifted performer in the Grand Prix firmament.

Michael had moved to Ferrari not only with a $25 million dollar retainer but with an avowed intention to help build Ferrari back up to the point where it could win its first Drivers' Championship crown since 1979. Yet in only the fourth race of the '96 season, Schumacher had a worrying taste of what he could expect from Villeneuve. The Canadian performed brilliantly under the most daunting pressure imaginable to win the European Grand Prix at the Nürburgring, crossing the line a scant 0.7 seconds ahead of reigning champion Schumacher's Ferrari, which had tailed him relentlessly for half the 67 lap race, waiting for the slip which never came.

It was a success which consolidated Jacques' second place in the World Championship points table, only 11 behind title leader Damon Hill, who battled hard after a poor start from pole position and could count himself fortunate to finish fourth, having slipped as low as 11th at one point during the early stages of the race.

In winning on only his fourth Grand Prix outing – and beating Schumacher in a straight fight – Villeneuve matched the achievement of the legendary Brazilian ace Emerson Fittipaldi, who achieved the same feat for Lotus in the 1970 United States Grand Prix. Only the late Giancarlo Baghetti, who won the 1961 French Grand Prix on his maiden outing, had bettered this achievement.

On his first visit to the spectacularly fast Spa-Francorchamps circuit for the 1996 Belgian Grand Prix, Villeneuve finished a strong second behind Schumacher's Ferrari. Then, during the Portuguese Grand Prix, Villeneuve overtook Schumacher round the *outside* of the flat-out right-hand corner before the pits. Michael smiled approvingly when questioned on this move at the post-race media conference. However, it would not take long for this indulgent attitude to change. If in 1996 Schumacher had regarded Villeneuve as something of an amusing newcomer, in 1997 he found himself up against the Canadian in a head-to-head battle for the World Championship.

Villeneuve began the season strongly, winning the Brazilian and Argentine Grands Prix to establish an early Championship lead. But then Schumacher won at Monaco, in Canada – where Jacques suffered the humiliation of spinning off in front of his home crowd – and then again in France. Villeneuve, who had managed an impressive victory in the Spanish Grand Prix, then added the British race to his list of victories before his form suddenly wobbled quite dramatically. He was lucky to win the Hungarian Grand Prix; then Schumacher triumphed brilliantly in Belgium for the second year running. It began to seem as though the title battle would go right down to the wire.

Snaring Schumacher had certainly been a major coup for Maranello, even though getting his signature on a contract blasted a substantial hole in the team's bank balance. Shell, Marlboro and Asprey all chipped in to make what was regarded all-round as a 22-carat investment. Unquestionably, it was the most sensible move the team had made since recruiting Alain Prost at the start of 1990.

The John Barnard-designed Ferrari F310 used torsion bar suspension front and rear in conjunction with pushrods and double wishbones and visual appearance highlighted by high-mounted elliptical ducting to radiator sidepods. This was a configuration which Barnard had originally adopted as long ago as 1989 on the type 640 which Nigel Mansell used to win on his Ferrari debut in Brazil. Barnard freely admitted that he would have been hard pressed to come up with any more effective system.

Schumacher's first experience of Ferrari motoring had come at the tail end of 1995 when he drove one of the existing V12 cars at Estoril, followed by a V12 chassis fitted with one of the new V10 engines. He was quite impressed with both those combinations, yet his initial assessment of the F310 was distinctly conservative. It was OK, he reckoned, but nothing in terms of a quantum leap forward.

'At Benetton the experience I had was that every year we got a new car, it was a step forward, a clear step forward. This did not happen with this year's Ferrari,' said Michael. 'In pure performance it wasn't really worse, but too survive in F1 you have to improve, to move forward. The step backwards was that it wasn't really quicker, but it was much more difficult to drive, much more difficult to handle and, in consistency, it was worse.

'But you never know, really, what is your car until you come to the races. The real problems of the car started to show out, not even so much in Melbourne, but from Brazil, Argentina onwards. Brazil was for us a disaster.'

Early problems with cracking of the titanium gearbox casing meant that the team had to muddle through the Brazilian and Argentine races with a 1995 rear end, complete with suspension and gearbox, fitted to the car, which badly compromised its performance. At least the new transverse six-speeder, suitably beefed up, was back on the car in time for the Nürburgring at the start of '96, where Schumacher drove superbly to shadow Villeneuve's winning Williams past the chequered flag. That was followed by a superb pole-winning performance at Imola and a strong run to second place. Nevertheless, the F310 was still demonstrating a degree of mechanical frailty. Just after taking pole for the San Marino race, Michael spun off when the rear suspension broke; and he was lucky to make it to the finish of the race in second place when a brake disc flew apart on the final lap.

Torrential rain at Barcelona provided the backdrop to an emotional first Schumacher/Ferrari triumph, but superman proved that he was human when he crashed the F310 on the first lap at Monaco and took its left front suspension off on the wall. It seemed like a harbinger of doom. For Canada, the Ferraris appeared in distinctive high-nose trim which did little for their aesthetics. Nor, indeed, their performance. It was the start of a dismal run. Irvine's car suffered a broken pushrod on the opening lap after Michael was forced to start at the back after suffering fuel pressure problems prior to the parade lap. He eventually retired when a driveshaft parted company with the car as he accelerated away after a refuelling stop.

At Magny-Cours, Schumacher was on pole again only for his V10 to suffer piston failure on the parade lap, while Irvine was out early on with a dicky hydraulic valve. Irvine reverted to a mechanical differential for Silverstone but succumbed to a bearing failure, while Schumacher stopped when a hydraulic manifold fitting on the gearbox worked loose and began leaking oil after only a couple of laps. This was getting ridiculous.

After the Monaco Grand Prix the strategy for the pit lane speed limiter was changed, and this seemed to trigger some peculiar torsional vibrations in the engine which led to gearbox oil pump failure on Irvine's car at both Hockenheim and Hungaroring. Michael finished fourth in front of his home crowd, then qualified on pole at Budapest, only to stop with electronic problems in the race.

At last, however, the tide seemed to turn, as Schumacher scored superb wins at Spa and Monza; he finished the year with a third (Estoril) and second (Suzuka) to pip Benetton for runner-up slot in the constructors' contest.

Other technical developments tried by Ferrari during the course of the year included a three-damper system in the front suspension, to help separate pitch from roll on the fast corners, and a slightly altered front wing. A steel-cased version of the transverse gearbox was introduced and a seven-speed version gradually developed.

At Monza the team went to greater extremes than just about anybody else in terms of a low downforce set-up and, although three of the new seven-speed gearboxes were now available, they were all earmarked for Schumacher's use and Eddie Irvine still had to rely on a six-speeder. You see, Michael was already taking the contractual initiative.

While Schumacher wrestled to come to terms with the Ferrari F310, Damon Hill was surging towards the 1996 World Championship crown at the wheel of his highly competitive Williams–Renault. Yet at Monza, a crucial mistake on the part of the British driver handed a great prize to Schumacher, Hill throwing away an easy Italian Grand Prix victory when he spun and stalled after clipping a makeshift tyre barrier at the exit of the first chicane at Monza.

The Englishman had just started his sixth lap and seemed well in control of proceedings, having strong-armed his way past Jean Alesi's fast-starting Benetton on the opening lap. Yet his luck was in. This was a day when title rival Jacques Villeneuve could only hobble home seventh, passing up a golden opportunity to move within striking distance of the World Championship lead. That allowed Ferrari team leader Michael Schumacher to race home to score Maranello's third Grand Prix victory of the season, delighting the 100,000-strong crowd who had been denied a home victory at Monza since 1988 when Gerhard Berger scored a fortuitous win after Ayrton Senna's McLaren tangled with Jean-Louis Schlesser while lapping the Williams stand-in during the closing stages.

Yet Michael was also lucky to escape a brush with potential disaster. With 13 laps left to run, he came within millimetres of duplicating Hill's fate when he too clipped the tyre wall at the first chicane.

'That was a stupid moment,' said the winner. 'I knew I had a big advantage in terms of times and had just been told by the pits to take it easy on the brakes. As I started to take things even easier, I just lost concentration and hit the tyre. I nearly lost control as the steering wheel snapped out of my hands.'

But even that heart-stopping moment when he almost failed to prevent the Ferrari 'tiller' from slipping through his hands hardly ruffled his composure. As the event drew to a close Schumacher rammed home his point with the race's fastest lap – 1 minute 26.110 seconds – only three laps from the chequered flag. He beat Alesi by 18.265 seconds, the Flying Finn Häkkinen another 48 seconds behind in third.

Ferrari finished the season on a high, its performance graph heading consistently skywards. At long, long last, a successor to Jody Scheckter as a Maranello-equipped World Champion seemed visible in the wings. Michael wound up a strong third in the Drivers' Championship on 59 points behind Hill (97) and Villeneuve (78), while the Italian team beat Benetton in the final race to secure the position of runner-up in the Constructors' Championship behind Williams.

It was a measure of just how much Michael Schumacher meant to Ferrari that by 1997 the Commendatore's old office building within the Fiorano test track had been converted to provide a flat and gymnasium for the German ace, to provide him with his own private accommodation whenever he visits Maranello.

Considering the extent of Ferrari's commitment to Schumacher, it obviously makes sense for the Prancing Horse to cosset its prime investment. Yet at the launch of the 1997 F1 Ferrari F310B, company president Luca di Montezemolo raised his sights only marginally. This year, said Luca, four race wins is the aim. The World Championship bid would take yet another year to materialize.

Schumacher felt much the same way. 'We expect reliability, we hope to win more races than we did,' he predicted; 'but to be honest, I think we won't really be able to win the Championship until 1998.'

Historians, of course, did not need reminding that this would be getting precariously close to the 20th anniversary of Jody Scheckter's 1979 World Championship – the last drivers' title to be won by Ferrari. To some, the current regime had at least provided stability and a sense of steady progression. Others felt that the promise of candy tomorrow had gone on just a little too long.

'This is a fairly conventional, standard F1 car upon which we tried different things with some surprises,' said John Barnard (who was to leave his post as Ferrari's R&D director mid-season to pursue other engineering projects as technical director for the rival Arrows squad).

'I feel very comfortable with this new car and it should be reliable, which is another reason why we have continued using the same gearbox for now. Easy to drive, stable and consistent are the qualities we have looked for in this car for 1997.'

Barnard's design also now favoured lower cockpit sides. The 1996 high-sided cockpit configuration caused problems with the efficiency of the engine airbox, forcing Schumacher and Irvine to cant their heads to one side on the straights in an effort to compensate.

The new car's garish livery reflected considerably increased Marlboro sponsorship, with continued additional backing from Shell, Pioneer, Asprey, Goodyear and Telecom Italia.

Paolo Martinelli's engine department had also worked very hard to develop an EV2 version of the 75-degree V10, 40-valve engine which the team hoped would be fully reliable after two months' testing prior to the first race in Melbourne.

Schumacher opened the new season with a second place in Australia behind David Coulthard's new McLaren–Mercedes MP4/12, was fifth in Brazil and then retired in Argentina after a first-corner collision. At Imola he was second again, chasing Heinz-Harald Frentzen's Williams hard all the way to the chequered flag, which he passed just 1.2 seconds behind his old rival. Then came an absolutely unforgettable performance to win in Monaco, surfing into the lead of the drivers' World Championship with a wet-weather victory every bit as decisive and commanding as his memorable 1996 performance at Barcelona.

Such was the magnitude of Schumacher's domination that he could even indulge in the luxury of a quick trip up the escape road at Ste Devote 53 laps into a race that was originally scheduled to run for 78 laps but ended up being flagged 16 laps ahead of schedule as the mandatory two hour cut-off point was reached. That little detour may have caused a few hearts to flutter among Ferrari personnel watching anxiously from the pit wall, but it cost Michael only 7.5 seconds over Rubens Barrichello's pursuing Stewart–Ford.

Ferrari's joy was compounded by Eddie Irvine's splendid run through from 15th on the grid to third at the chequered flag, but their satisfaction was as nothing compared with the delight in the Stewart–Ford camp as Barrichello came home a brilliant third on only the team's fifth Grand Prix outing, posting the best finish so far for Bridgestone in the process.

Schumacher played it shrewdly from the start, trying both a dry and intermediate chassis set-up immediately before the off. At the last possible moment, he switched to the spare F310B using an intermediate set-up on Goodyear's intermediate tyre choice. He was 6.6 seconds ahead on the opening lap, then stretched his advantage to 11.5, 15.7, 16.7 and 22.1 seconds the next four times round.

By then the race was won. Such was his advantage, it was of almost academic interest that he switched to a set of Goodyear's 1996 spec 'quattro' full rain tyres at his sole refuelling stop on lap 32. Many of his fellow Goodyear runners tried the latest hand-cut vee-pattern '97 wet and, by common consensus, this didn't have quite the same level of bite.

It was the start of a trend. Schumacher scored a fortuitous victory in the Canadian Grand Prix at Montreal, a race that was dominated by David Coulthard's McLaren but was stopped early after Olivier Panis crashed heavily in his Prost–Peugeot, breaking both his legs. He went on to win the French Grand Prix at Magny-Cours, then retired at Silverstone and took second and fourth at Hockenheim and Budapest before posting a spectacularly driven victory at Spa-Francorchamps

However, September 1997 looked set to be recalled in the pages of F1 history as the month which saw Ferrari crash out of the 1997 World Championship race after one of the most disastrous reversals of fortune in recent motor racing history. Nobody who left Spa-Francorchamps on 24 August after Michael Schumacher's majestic victory in the Belgian Grand Prix could have imagined that the next three races would yield the German ace just a paltry two World Championship points.

Simultaneously, Jacques Villeneuve and the Williams team produced an impressive reversal of form to win both the Austrian and Luxembourg Grands Prix. Adding these results to his two points for fifth at Monza, he scored a total of 22 points, catapulting himself into a nine-point lead with only two races left to run.

Ferrari's nightmare began at Monza where Schumacher could only scrape home sixth, unable to optimize his F310B's handling all weekend. His only consolation was that Villeneuve also had an off-day, finishing once place ahead of him on the road.

Two weeks later, in the first Austrian Grand Prix to be held in a decade, Michael found himself the recipient of a

10-second 'stop–go' penalty after overtaking Heinz-Harald Frentzen's Williams when a yellow flag was being waved, after a collision between Eddie Irvine's Ferrari and Jean Alesi's Benetton. As a result, Schumacher finished fifth behind younger brother Ralf's Jordan, rather than in the second place behind Villeneuve which he originally predicted was a feasible ambition.

One week later, at the Nürburgring for the Luxembourg Grand Prix, the Schumacher brothers featured centre stage in the most embarrassing fashion imaginable. On the sprint to the first corner, Michael saw the flickering embers of his title challenge all but extinguished as Ralf's over-exuberance triggered a multi-car collision. Schumacher junior, who'd qualified his Jordan in eighth place, came hurtling down the outside of his brother going into the first corner, then cut across to swing into the right-hander absolutely wheel-to-wheel with his team-mate Giancarlo Fisichella.

Having squeezed Fisichella up the kerb, Ralf then bounced back across the Ferrari's right front wheel, just as Michael was endeavouring to get out of the way by steering straight across the gravel trap. Leaving the two Jordan drivers to sort out their differences at the side of the circuit, Michael limped into the pits at the end of the second lap. One quick glance and the F310B was pushed away with deranged right front suspension.

Dan Gurney's remarks after the multi-car shunt at the start of the 1966 Indy 500 immediately sprang to many people's lips: 'Why a group of the world's top racing drivers cannot drive down a straight piece of road without running into each other is beyond me.' Or was it, as some said, just a racing accident?

Others in the paddock felt the younger Schumacher should be reminded that, simply because he has a famous surname, he does not have automatic access to track space already occupied by other competitors.

Under the circumstances, Michael controlled his disappointment with admirable reserve. 'After my brother Ralf hit me, my car was handling strangely,' he said. 'I did not know if it was a puncture or some other problem with my tyres. When I came into the pits, it was obvious that a suspension arm was bent and I had to retire.' The race was only two laps old.

The other big news to emerge from this trio of races was the emergence of McLaren–Mercedes as Formula One's pace-setters. David Coulthard drove superbly to win the Italian Grand Prix at Monza, neatly vaulting ahead of Alesi's Benetton at their sole scheduled refuelling stop. Thanks to a new front wing developed by McLaren's recently appointed technical chief Adrian Newey, the McLaren MP4/12s now offered drivers Coulthard and Mika Häkkinen a reassuringly crisp element of front-end bite. Gone was the touch of understeer which had previously frustrated both men, and Häkkinen was at last able to place his dynamic talent on very public display.

The Finn qualified second to Villeneuve in Austria, then took the first pole of his 94-race F1 career at the Nürburgring the following weekend. Yet both races ended in acute disappointment for the McLaren–Merc squad. Mika retired with engine failure, while leading at the end of the opening lap at the A1-Ring; then both he and Coulthard suffered very public blow-ups under the noses of the Mercedes top brass at the Luxembourg Grand Prix after running in dominant

1–2 fashion for much of the race. That left the way clear for a remarkable Renault 1–2–3–4 grand slam with Alesi (Benetton), Frentzen (Williams) and Gerhard Berger (Benetton) following Villeneuve past the chequered flag.

At the end of the race, Ferrari sporting director Jean Todt accused McLaren of running a 'torque modulation' system which, although given the green light by the FIA, did not, in his view, conform to the spirit of the regulations. This elicited a frosty response from McLaren boss Ron Dennis, who treated the remarks with lofty disdain.

The way Ferrari tech chief Ross Brawn tells it, the advantage of the current Maranello V10's comparatively flat torque curve has been negated by the allowing of such systems which soften the peaky power delivery of not only the Mercedes engine, but also the Renault V10s used by Williams. 'We believe this is against the spirit of the regulations, and we do not accept it,' said Todt.

The biggest controversy came in the Japanese Grand Prix where Villeneuve was excluded from the meeting after allegedly failing to slow down when the yellow warning flags were displayed during a practice session.

The Williams team appealed against this penalty, so Jacques was permitted to start the race. Having qualified on pole position, he accelerated into an immediate lead and drove deliberately slowly to keep the pack boxed in tightly behind him. With Schumacher in second place, Jacques might have been forgiven for thinking that an over-exuberant rival would make a bid to overtake the Ferrari and knock off his rival, innocently, of course. In the event, Schumacher went on to win the race thanks in part to some questionable assistance from team-mate Eddie Irvine. Villeneuve eventually finished fifth, ostensibly facing the final round of the World Championship just one point ahead of Schumacher.

But the FIA Court of Appeal rejected the Williams team's appeal and Jacques was disqualified, losing the two points which accrued for fifth place. Now he was one point behind Schumacher going into the last race of the season, the European Grand Prix at Jeréz in southern Spain.

The two title rivals went to the starting line amid a mood of enormous tension and expectancy. Villeneuve's pole position was on the cleaner left-hand side of the circuit, but many people predicted that Schumacher was more favourably placed on the right-hand side of the track, aiming for the first right-hander. And so it proved.

'I wasn't on new tyres from the start of the race and I had to struggle to keep up with Michael,' said Villeneuve. 'At the start he was simply glued to the asphalt. I don't know how he did it. I was impressed, because I was sliding everywhere.

'Then he was on the inside of me going into the first corner after the start and my team-mate Heinz-Harald Frentzen came up on the inside of me and I gave him room because I didn't want to risk banging wheels with him at this early stage in the race.'

By the end of the opening lap Schumacher was 1.9 seconds ahead of Frentzen, with Villeneuve third in front of the McLaren-Mercedes of Mika Häkkinen and David Coulthard. It took until lap eight for Jacques to go ahead of his team-mate to take second place, after which the Williams team leader immediately steadied the Ferrari's advantage at 4.2 seconds, fading slightly to 4.7 seconds by lap 12.

On lap 22 tension was heightened dramatically as Schumacher made his first refuelling stop in 7.6 seconds, resuming fourth behind Villeneuve, Frentzen and Häkkinen. Now the race became acutely tactical. On lap 23 Villeneuve made his first refuelling stop, dropping down the order to fifth behind Coulthard.

On lap 25 Coulthard obligingly pulled in from fourth place to make his first refuelling stop, which allowed Villeneuve to pull up on to Schumacher's Ferrari. On lap 26 Häkkinen made his first stop, then Frentzen headed for the pit lane on lap 28 and, hey presto, Schumacher and Villeneuve were back in first and second places, separated by only 0.9 of a second.

Since his first stop, Villeneuve had been on fresh rubber and was now piling on the pressure. From 3.1 seconds behind the gap came down to 2.0 seconds on lap 35, then 1.7 seconds on lap 40. Ralf Schumacher, running the spare Jordan, did his bit to help big brother as they lapped the Peugeot-engined car on lap 40, but it only cost Villeneuve 0.4 seconds. Now everybody was on tenterhooks anticipating the second round of refuelling stops.

Schumacher made his second stop at the end of lap 43, followed by Villeneuve a lap later. Again the Williams driver got back into the race third behind Coulthard, but again the McLaren driver cleared the way by coming in for his second stop next time round.

Now Villeneuve was all over Schumacher's rear wing and lunged for the inside line going into Dry Sack, the sixth corner of the lap. Then the two cars collided.

'I knew I had to make my move them, or else my tyres would go off a bit, lose grip and I wouldn't be able to fight anymore,' said Villeneuve. 'I just went for it, and just braked late. I was surprised that he hadn't closed the door yet, but it was only a matter of seconds before he decided to turn in on me. But he didn't do it well enough, because he went out and I didn't.

'The impact was very hard. The way we banged wheels was hard enough to break my suspension. It was not a small thing, but the car felt strange and I took the next few laps pretty slowly. Once I was sure that the suspension was not touching the tyre I managed to press on intermittently, but the car felt odd on right-hand corners.'

Schumacher's Ferrari, unable to drag itself back on to the tarmac, was left beached in the gravel trap, along with its driver's World Championship hopes. Despite concerns that his car had sustained quite serious damage, Villeneuve was left to battle poor handling and unpredictable tyre wear for the remainder of the distance, eventually capitulating to the challenge of Häkkinen and Coulthard who came through to score a McLaren–Mercedes 1–2 in the closing moments of the race.

After the race both Schumacher and Villeneuve were summoned to the stewards to offer their explanations of the collision. It was eventually decided that this was a racing accident, but 24 hours later – after Schumacher had reaped a whirlwind of vitriolic criticism, particularly from the Italian and German media – the FIA stepped in to summon the Ferrari driver to appear before an extraordinary meeting of its World Council on 11 November.

The net result of these deliberations was to leave the sport's governing body fielding a barrage of complaint. For the World Council indeed found Schumacher guilty of deliberately running into Jacques Villeneuve in the European Grand Prix, but then let him off with a superficial slap over the wrists.

Motor racing insiders were amazed when the FIA President Max Mosley announced that the Ferrari driver would merely be excluded from the results of the 1997 World Championship, while his race results achieved throughout the year would remain on the record book. It was also part of the deal that he would take part in a European Union road safety campaign in 1998. There was no mention of a fine, race ban or possible loss of points at the start of the 1998 season. Many felt that he had been let off the hook far too leniently. Yet Mosley brushed aside such criticism, insisting that it was important to create a firm deterrent which would prevent a repeat of such behaviour in the future.

'The World Council has come to the conclusion that although Michael Schumacher acted deliberately, it was instinctive and it was not premeditated,' he said. 'Careful thought was given to banning him for 1998, but it has concluded that to do so would be futile because there is no driver competing in 1998 who would not be ready to accept a ban in 1999 if he could win the championship in 1998. So it would not be a deterrent in any sense.'

Mosley explained that it was necessary to consider what might have happened if Villeneuve, who went on to finish third in the European Grand Prix, had retired as a result of his collision with Schumacher. The German driver would have then won the championship.

'The right thing to do [under those circumstances] would have been to disqualify Schumacher and Villeneuve would have been champion,' he said. 'That is the fundamental point.

'It is a very serious thing to lose a vice-championship. But, most important of all, it sends a message to drivers at all levels in the sport, that if you do something you shouldn't do when the championship is in issue, you will be excluded from that championship and you cannot possibly gain anything from indulging in an illegitimate act.'

Mosley's explanations failed to silence the chorus of disapproval over the FIA's decision among the sport's leading names. Jackie Stewart, the three times World Champion whose F1 team had made its debut this season, admitted that he was surprised that Schumacher had received such mild treatment.

'Yes, I think he has got off lightly,' he said. 'He is a very lucky boy. I personally felt that the effect the incident had on the sport alone was very damaging on a global basis. I firmly believe he should have been made an example of.'

Jody Scheckter, Ferrari's previous World Champion driver who had taken the laurels in 1979, agreed. 'It surprised me very much that the penalty was not more severe,' he said. 'You can't deliberately try and knock people off in F1, it is just too dangerous. My guess would have been that he should had a three-race ban next season. This is not what F1 should be about.'

Williams Technical Director Patrick Head remained philosophical. 'We didn't wish for any ban,' he said. 'But we are well aware that Ferrari and the FIA are very close.'

Veteran F1 team owner Ken Tyrrell laughed ironically. 'I have heard what has happened and I am still waiting for somebody to tell me what punishment he received,' he joked. 'Really, he hasn't had any punishment. It is no penalty.'

On a different note, the World Council dismissed any charges of collusion between the McLaren and Williams teams after allegations that they had conspired to fix the result of the European Grand Prix. All agreed the FIA had made the right decision. On this issue at least.

Unquestionably, Schumacher was rocked by the FIA World Council decision. Up until then, the German *Wunderkind* had seemingly led a charmed life as a member of Grand Prix motor racing's elite. Now, not only had he been beaten by a relative newcomer, but his own behaviour had been judged by the sport's rulers to be seriously lacking.

Michael tried to brush the matter aside, saying that the incident at Jeréz had not spoiled his good personal relationship with Villeneuve. After all, he pointed out, they'd been out for a beer together on the evening after the race. Things couldn't be that bad.

Villeneuve saw it differently. 'We're not close friends, nor ever will be,' he insisted. 'All this stuff about us being close is just rubbish. It's not true. Michael is a good driver, but he's certainly not unbeatable. And I believe that I can continue to beat him in 1998.'

Everything had changed. Now there was talk that the new World Champion was poised to move his career up a notch. No longer just the blond kid in the best car, shaking a stick at Michael Schumacher. Suddenly he had become the man who might – just might – have the nerve to topple the Ferrari driver from his perceived position atop the F1 pile. But by the time the 1998 season had started, all this seemed to have been forgotten. Indeed, more people were talking about the domination of the two McLaren team drivers than about Michael Schumacher.

Chapter Five

Time to deliver

Ferrari's firm assertion that nothing less than winning the World Championship would do in 1998 threatened to hang like an albatross round the neck of the Italian team's Sporting Director Jean Todt almost from the outset. Ever since the new Ferrari F300 was unveiled before Christmas, Todt had set his sights understandably high, although his words also reflected a tacit acknowledgement that his future with the team could be on the line if Michael Schumacher were not given the equipment to get the job done.

Ferrari had come closer to winning the title in 1997 than anyone – not excepting charismatic President Luca di Montezemolo – had expected, even if the inelegant collision between Schumacher and Jacques Villeneuve in the final race of the season ended the season on an unsatisfactory note. Yet there were many within the F1 community who believed that the famous Italian team had missed a crucial window of opportunity and that its prospects of a title crown in the foreseeable future had ended in the gravel trap at Jeréz together with Schumacher's car.

'We've seen very little of Ferrari [testing] at similar tracks to other people,' said Williams Technical Director Patrick Head prior to the start of the '98 season. 'It's probably a good decision, because there's always a lot of pressure on Ferrari, but this year they seem deliberately to have put pressure on themselves by saying "There are no excuses this year."

'I suspect they may be scrabbling for an excuse when they get to Melbourne, but I don't know they will go over a full season. I'm not sure Ferrari are totally unconfident, if you like, but I'm not certain they are quite as confident as they were when they first announced their new car.'

The tantalizing element of uncertainty surrounding the F300's prospects had been heightened by the fact that Ferrari had shied away from a head-to-head confrontation with its rivals during winter testing ever since the new car ran for the first time in late December. While most UK-based teams limbered up with their new cars at Silverstone and then joined in the free-for-all sessions at Barcelona, Ferrari stayed away. The team preferred to do its development work either at the twisting little Fiorano test track adjacent to its headquarters at Maranello, or at the Ferrari-owned Mugello circuit near Florence. As only a handful of other teams use Mugello for F1 testing, so it was impossible to gain an accurate barometer of the new Ferrari's progress.

Chief Designer Rory Byrne and Technical Director Ross Brawn had impressive enough technical credentials, having previously crafted the Benettons with which Schumacher won the World Championship in 1994 and 95, but the F300 was the first Ferrari they had designed together.

The new car was lighter, lower and more aerodynamically efficient than its predecessor, designed by John Barnard before he left Ferrari. The team also remained contracted to run on Goodyear tyres at a time when rivals Bridgestone, who supplied McLaren, Benetton, Arrows, Stewart, Prost and Minardi, had been demonstrating a firm performance edge.

It was obviously difficult for Brawn and Byrne to adapt their own design philosophy round a car which had originally been conceived by another engineer. Yet, by the same token, that gave the two men a ready-made excuse to fall back on if the Ferrari failed to match the pace set by its key rivals from Williams and McLaren. This year they started with a clean sheet of paper and had no such excuse.

Schumacher, meanwhile, believed he had atoned for the collision with Villeneuve which had ended the previous year's championship battle on such a controversial note. Yet although the German driver seemed coolly confident, the Ferrari team radiated none of the thinly suppressed high-tension excitement one could detect at McLaren, nor the quietly understated confidence of Williams.

'The only reason I could see for things not going well is if we have big reliability problems, are really unlucky or because of the tyre situation which is very difficult to predict,' said Schumacher. 'If you have a situation, like we did sometimes last year, when one tyre make is a second a lap faster than the other, what can you do?'

By the time he reached the third round of the Championship, all eyes were on Schumacher again at Buenos Aires. Michael emerged victorious from the Argentine Grand Prix after a controversial race which saw him not only elbow David Coulthard aside in unruly fashion during the opening phase of the race, but beat Mika Häkkinen fair and square in a sprint to the chequered flag.

Häkkinen's second place on a circuit he dislikes at least kept him comfortably in the lead of the Drivers' World Championship, but for Coulthard the race turned out to be a disaster. When the starting signal was given David accelerated cleanly into the lead from pole position, with Häkkinen taking second place from Schumacher as the pack funnelled into the first long right-hander. At the end of the opening lap the order was Coulthard, Häkkinen, Schumacher, then Heinz-Harald Frentzen's Williams FW20, Eddie Irvine in the other Ferrari F300, Jacques Villeneuve's Williams and Jean Alesi's Sauber C17.

However, any hopes that the McLarens might make an early break were dashed when Schumacher went ahead of Häkkinen to take second place midway round the second lap, Irvine emphasizing the Ferrari threat by displacing Frentzen from fourth at almost the same point. The German driver's Williams had lost a front wing end plate on the formation lap and was suffering a dramatic handling imbalance as a result, making it difficult for him to sustain a consistent pace.

Now Schumacher was after Coulthard with a vengeance. On lap four David went slightly wide entering the slow right-hand hairpin at the end of the back straight, and repeated this slip at the same point next time round. Schumacher saw his opportunity, heaving his Ferrari's inside wheels up the kerb as he scrabbled round the inside. Coulthard tightened his line and the two cars collided, the silver McLaren–Mercedes being launched into a half-spin over the left front wheel of its rival.

'I didn't feel obliged to lift off because I had the momentum,' said Schumacher, 'then David closed the door on me and we touched.'

Coulthard resumed in 12th place, eventually climbing back to sixth at the chequered flag: quite an achievement considering he was briefly rammed off the circuit by Jacques Villeneuve's Williams during their battle for seventh place.

A detailed analysis of the situation inevitably cast another shadow of doubt over Coulthard's vulnerability under pressure. Braking hard for this hairpin, Coulthard found the downchange mechanism on his McLaren–Mercedes' gearbox 'balking' slightly. This fault meant that the car was slightly late in selecting the lower gear, with the result that he ran slightly wide from the apex of the right-hand corner. Sensing his opportunity, Schumacher pounced.

'It is unusual for drivers to collide on the exit to a corner,' said Coulthard quizzically. 'Usually it is on the entry and I was still a metre and a half ahead of Michael, so I just held my line. I think he was just expecting me to drive out of his way, or else he was just prepared to sit there and see what happened. I think Michael was being a bit aggressive, but I am thankful that at least I was driving a strong car.'

Schumacher retorted: 'David had run wide at that corner the lap before. I didn't want to slow my pace and lose time, so I went down the inside and then he shut the door.'

Coulthard exacted his revenge by beating Michael into second place in the San Marino Grand Prix, but then Häkkinen won again in Spain and at Monaco, the Finn receiving a double bonus in the latter event when Schumacher produced an uncharacteristically erratic performance which ended on lap 30 when he got involved in a vigorous barging match with Alexander Wurz's Benetton as they battled for second place.

As they lapped a group of slower cars, Schumacher dived for the inside line under braking for the first-gear Loews hairpin; but Wurz had no intention of being intimidated into giving way, stayed with the Ferrari on the outside line and then cheekily repassed into the next right-hander.

Schumacher was clearly caught off-balance by his rival's audacity and barged back inside the Benetton to take second place as they accelerated out on to the waterfront. Unfortunately, as he did so, he hit Wurz quite hard, bending a left rear suspension link on the Ferrari which immediately forced him into the pits.

After an initial inspection, Schumacher's initial reaction was to climb out of the cockpit. However, Ross Brawn instructed him to get back in immediately and refasten his belts while the mechanics worked methodically to repair the damage. Häkkinen had lapped him three times by the time the Ferrari driver accelerated back into the race, now firmly in last position and with very little hope of making up for lost time.

Meanwhile Wurz came in for his refuelling stop at the end of lap 42, resuming third behind team-mate Fisichella only to crash at high speed next time round through the tunnel. The Benetton team speculated that the accident might have been caused by damage sustained in the brush with Schumacher; or the young Austrian may have just pushed too hard on cold tyres. Either way, he was lucky to escape harm in his 170 mph impact against the barrier.

Meanwhile, Schumacher was back in the chase. This relentless grind of Monaco imposes great technical strain on the cars, and usually produces more than its fair share of mechanical casualties. With that in mind, Schumacher clearly hoped that perhaps a single championship point for sixth place might conceivably be within his grasp.

In fact, despite lapping consistently quickly on his return to the fray, Schumacher made little progress on the cars in front and finally settled for tenth, knocking his car's front wing off against Pedro Diniz's Arrows on the final lap. By any

Getting ready for the big time. Schumacher's debut with Jordan – at Spa in 1991 – was so impressive that Benetton stepped in and signed him up for the remainder of the season.

Right, the 1993 Ford-powered Benetton B193B – pictured here at the Hungaroring – netted Schumi just the one GP victory, at Estoril, in a season when Williams was dominant.

Left, Schumacher quickly established himself in the F1 community and as number one driver at Benetton – thanks to excellent performances on the track and to sound political guidance from his manager Willi Weber *(below)*.

OMGE
GOODYEAR
SUGARFREE
5

Above, with Ayrton Senna tragically killed at Imola in 1994, Schumacher and Benetton became the dominant force in Formula 1 for the next two seasons.

Below, Damon Hill – picking up the mantle for Williams – was the only driver who consistently put Schumi under pressure. Their rivalry was excellent copy for the tabloid press.

Above, joining Ferrari in 1996, Schumacher set about transforming the team's fortunes until he and team mate Eddie Irvine became regular visitors to the podium.

Below, brilliant wet weather drives – such as this one at Monaco in 1997 – have established the German as one of the all-time greats.

Above, Schumi scored an unusual victory at Silverstone in 1998 – crossing the finish line (in first place) in the pits in order to serve a 10-second penalty.

Below, so near and yet… for two consecutive years – 1997 and 1998 – Schumacher lost the World Championship at the last race. But he showed no signs of giving up.

Right, a keen footballer, he continues to play regularly for his local club in Germany.

N2
ENNEDUE

Above, the accident at Silverstone in 1999 had echoes of Imola '94,
but Schumacher was back on top form for the final two races of the year.

Below, as the year 2000 dawned – and another championship challenge for Ferrari –
his legs were clearly back to full strength.

standards, it was a deeply unconvincing performance from the three times Monaco winner.

'If we really fail to make more progress in terms of our competitive performance by the next race in Canada, our chances of winning the World Championship will have gone,' said Schumacher firmly.

In fact, the Montreal race enabled Michael to bounce back into contention for Championship with a spectacular victory, surviving two routine refuelling stops and an extra visit to the pit lane for a 10-second stop–go penalty after pushing his compatriot Heinz-Harald Frentzen off the circuit when he was accelerating back into the race after his first visit to the pit lane.

Yet hardly had Schumacher descended from the rostrum than he launched into a bitter and somewhat over-emotional tirade against his old rival Damon Hill, accusing the Englishman of trying to push him off the circuit as they battled for second place on lap 38.

'You don't want to hear the words I thought at that moment,' said Schumacher, 'because that was purely dangerous. If someone wants to kill you, he can do it in a different way, because going down there [the straight before the pits] you are doing 180 mph and moving off-line three times is impossible.

'I was so angry that I wondered why he did not get a penalty for that. I will be having a big word with him.'

By the same token, Schumacher excused himself from the incident with Frentzen, remarking, 'If it was my fault, I apologize, but I just didn't see him at all.'

Frentzen saw it differently. 'He's the guy who is always complaining about people coming out of the pits and moving straight onto the racing line,' he fumed. 'I am really angry about what he did.'

Meanwhile, David Coulthard's hopes of closing the gap on his McLaren team-mate Mika Häkkinen at the head of the points table sustained another frustrating broadside in an action-packed race as both the Mercedes-engined cars retired with rare mechanical trouble, handing Michael Schumacher and Ferrari a fast lane through to their second victory in seven races so far this season.

Schumacher, who beat Giancarlo Fisichella's Benetton into second place after a spirited showing by the young Italian star, now split the McLaren drivers in the title stakes. After a race which for much of its distance seemed to have degenerated into a destruction derby, Schumacher was now 12 points behind Häkkinen, but five ahead of the luckless Coulthard.

After several laps Coulthard managed to stabilize his advantage over the pursuing Ferrari, but this was abruptly dissipated when the safety car was deployed for a second time between laps 14 and 17 after Arrows driver Pedro Diniz spun off and then resumed, scattering clods of earth and grass all round the circuit as he did so.

On lap 19 Coulthard suddenly slowed and the second McLaren trailed gently round to the pits to retire with a throttle problem, allowing Schumacher through into the lead.

Then came the incident with Frentzen which left Fisichella's Benetton leading from Villeneuve who, next time round, promptly lunged across the same gravel trap which had claimed Frentzen. He just managed to get back on the track, only to be hit from behind by Esteban Tuero's Minardi, resulting in the local hero spending four laps in the pits having the Williams's rear wing replaced.

This left Schumacher chasing Fisichella for the lead, but Michael had to come in for his 10 second stop–go penalty for his treatment of Frentzen at the end of lap 35. That put Fisichella ahead again; but Schumacher went back in front for good when the Benetton made its refuelling stop at the end of lap 44.

Michael returned across the Atlantic to win the French Grand Prix at Magny-Cours, but only after the race was stopped and restarted when a slower car stalled on the grid. Häkkinen's McLaren got away best at the first start, but Schumacher did a better job second time round and ran away with the race as a result.

'Sometimes the playing field doesn't seem level, and this is one of those times,' noted McLaren Managing Director Ron Dennis after Schumacher and Irvine firmly beat his best-placed car, driven by Mika Häkkinen, into third place. The notion that the official starter had decided to give Ferrari a second chance after Häkkinen beat Schumacher off the line at the first attempt may be regarded by outsiders as evidence that acute paranoia is alive and well within the Grand Prix community.

However, it is a measure of the internal strains and rivalries among the top teams in this high-pressure business that such ideas are even aired in public. Formula One is a highly politicized world, and ever since Schumacher was let off with a nominal wrist-slapping for attempting to ram Jacques Villeneuve off the circuit in the 1997 Championship clincher at Jeréz, an air of unease over what many regarded as the FIA's partiality towards the Italian team had pervaded the paddocks.

None of this altered the fact that Schumacher's winning performance proved that Ferrari was now firmly established as a consistently formidable F1 operator. It was easy to argue that Häkkinen might have dominated the race had he got away in the lead at the second start – but he didn't. That was the fact of the matter.

Moreover, Ferrari's success received personal praise from the company's high-profile president Luca di Montezemolo. Having telephoned the Circuit de Nevers to congratulate his team personally on that Sunday's result, he also confirmed that Sporting Director Jean Todt had renewed his contract to remain in his current role until the end of the 2001 World Championship season.

Todt's decision to stay on at Ferrari will provide a hitherto undreamed-of level of management stability within the most famous team in the F1 business. It was also likely to have been a major factor in tempting Schumacher to sign a further long-term contract with the team beyond the end of the 1999 season.

Since 1993 Todt, the ascetic Frenchman who had previously masterminded the Le Mans winning Peugeot sports car team, had transformed Ferrari from a chaotic group of warring factions into a front-line fighting force. 'This is a dream result,' said Todt after the French race. 'Schumacher and Irvine had an incredible race and Eddie did a great job to keep the McLarens behind him.'

As if that were not enough, Michael went on to ensure that F1 grabbed the headlines on World Cup final night by scoring his first ever British Grand Prix victory, although yet again a whirlwind of controversy surrounded events at Silverstone.

Having won a remarkable high-speed battle with Mika Häkkinen's McLaren on a track surface intermittently assailed by torrential rain, Schumacher brought his Ferrari

F300 into the pit lane to take a 10-second stop–go penalty *after* it had actually passed the chequered flag to take the race. This was the culmination of a sequence of events which meant the race ended in a state of considerable bad feeling and tension, with McLaren lodging an official protest over the way the matter was handled which was still being debated some time later .

Schumacher had earlier allegedly passed the Benetton of Alexander Wurz on lap 43 of the 60-lap race while the field was queued up behind the safety car which had been deployed to slow the pace of the race during the height of the downpour. For this rule transgression the 29-year-old German driver was penalized with a 10-second stop–go penalty, but the stewards decided that this should be added to his race time rather than bringing him into the pits for a more time-consuming delay. However, according to the rules, adding 10 seconds to the elapsed race time can only be applied if the race is within 12 laps of the finish, which this clearly was not.

Before the safety car went out, Häkkinen's McLaren–Mercedes had built up a 38-second lead over Schumacher, only to see this dissipated as the field slowed to a comparative crawl and Schumacher fell into line behind Giancarlo Fisichella's Benetton and Toronosuke Takagi's Tyrrell in the queue behind the silver Mercedes. Two laps before the safety car emerged, Häkkinen had spun wildly across the grass and a gravel trap on the outside of Bridge Corner – a 150 mph, near-flat-out right-hander in dry conditions – but managed to recover control and rejoin the circuit beyond the next corner.

After five laps' slow crawl, the pack was unleashed and Schumacher moved in for the kill. With his nose section damaged by that spin over the grass, Häkkinen was now struggling with a handling imbalance that prevented him fending off the Ferrari, which surged past into the lead on lap 51.

Even Schumacher admitted he had been lucky. 'I probably only won because of the safety car and Mika's problems,' he said 'but I have to say that I just did not see the yellow flag for the Benetton which I was supposed to have passed.'

Schumacher's maiden British F1 victory left him trailing Championship leader Häkkinen by just two points, but for David Coulthard the race was an absolute disaster, his title hopes literally sunk for good when he spun out of second place during the heaviest of the rain.

More controversy, more backlash. It seemed to be the same story all over again. In the days after the race FIA President Max Mosley again found himself prompted into vigorously denying rumours that Ferrari and its number one driver were being favoured.

'Anyone who looks at all the races [this year] would realize that there is no conspiracy,' said Mosley. 'Take the Canadian Grand Prix where the race was stopped and restarted. You could say that Schumacher was disadvantaged on this occasion, as he was second at the first start and then third at the second. But it is just not the case.'

Mosley would not be drawn into commenting on the issues involved at Silverstone, as McLaren's appeal against the rejection of their protest was still to be heard. Nor would McLaren's Managing Director Ron Dennis add anything to the debate; but it was clear that the main plank of his team's appeal centred on apparent ambiguities and inconsistencies in the sequence of events that took place at Silverstone that Sunday afternoon.

Schumacher was running third on lap 43 when he lapped Wurz's sixth-placed Benetton under a stationary yellow flag. This incident took place at 3.15 p.m. and the safety car was deployed to slow the field in heavy rain only one minute later. However, the stewards did not get round to deliberating on the matter until 3.39 p.m., and the Ferrari team timed its receipt of the decision that a 'time penalty' of 10 seconds had been imposed at 3.46 p.m. By this time there were only three laps to go before the end of the race and, in order to produce a symbolic compliance with the instruction, Schumacher came in to take his stop–go penalty on lap 60, just *after* taking the chequered flag.

'When the official handed us the document relating to the penalty, he was unable to tell us which rule it referred to,' said Jean Todt, Ferrari's Sporting Director. 'Because of this doubt we brought Michael in for a stop–go penalty in conformity with the regulation allowing you to make the stop within three laps of its notification.'

When the results were published it was clear that the organizers had simply added ten seconds to Schumacher's elapsed race time, giving him the win by 12 seconds. In fact, because the race was not into its final 12 laps by the time of the rule infringement, Schumacher should have been brought into the pits for a 10-second stop–go penalty, a punishment which would have cost him more of his advantage when the 'in' and 'out' lap are also taken into account.

McLaren's view was that this was unfair and amounted to preferential treatment to the Ferrari team. What they wanted to know was just why it took so long to advise Ferrari of the penalty in the first place – and why the penalty imposed on Schumacher was not displayed on the timing monitors. This was an absolutely crucial omission, as the rules say that the three laps of grace during which the 10 seconds stop–go penalty must be taken only start running from the moment the message '10 seconds stop–go penalty' appears on the screen alongside the driver's name. Sources close to the FIA concede that the initial evidence points to the race stewards making a major error of judgement in applying the rules, mitigated in part by race control's pre-occupation in monitoring the safety car's progress in slowing the field in the most dangerous period of heavy rain during the middle of the race.

Michael then finished third in Austria, given a leg-up by Irvine who did not resist an overtaking move in the closing moments of the race, and was lucky to emerge from his home race at Hockenheim an off-the-pace fifth.

Then came a brilliant tactical win on the twisting Hungaroring circuit, near Budapest. Schumacher scored his fifth Ferrari victory of the season here in surroundings where a lack of overtaking opportunities meant making the most of an astute, well-judged refuelling strategy as important as relentless determination behind the wheel.

Ferrari switched from a two-stop to a three-stop strategy, concluding as the race unfolded that this would be the quickest route to complete the gruelling 77-lap distance on the harder of the two available Goodyear tyre compounds. After Michael had qualified third, he certainly needed some creative means of vaulting ahead of the fast qualifying McLaren–Mercs; and the whole game plan paid off magnificently. When he emerged from his third pit visit just 5 seconds ahead of David Coulthard's MP4/13, the day was complete and all he had to do was simply cruise home to victory ahead of the Scot.

'It was very much a race run at qualifying speed throughout for me,' said Schumacher, admitting he did not make the decision to change from a two-stop to a three-stop strategy until he had refuelled for the first time on lap 25.

'We [finally] employed a three-stop strategy, which was pretty difficult, and it didn't seem to be working out at the beginning, because I fell behind Jacques Villeneuve at the first pit stop.

'Ross Brawn [the Ferrari Technical Director] took the decision what to do and told me what the strategy was after that first stop, but as I was sitting behind Jacques, I was wondering whether it was the right thing.' It certainly was!

That victory in Hungary looked set to be the springboard from which Schumacher could consolidate his World Championship challenge. Yet the Belgian Grand Prix which followed a fortnight later saw Michael in even more trouble.

Damon Hill won the race to post the Jordan F1 team's maiden Grand Prix victory, but while the British veteran basked in the afterglow of what would prove to be the last win of his own career, Schumacher was at the centre of a whirlwind of controversy after his leading Ferrari crashed into the back of Coulthard's McLaren as he came up to lap the Scot, subsequently three-wheeling back to the pits. He thereby squandered a golden opportunity to seize the Championship points lead from Mika Häkkinen, whose McLaren had spun into retirement on the first corner of the restarted race. Schumacher reacted to the incident in a fit of rage, leaping from his damaged car in the pit lane and storming up to the McLaren pit where mechanics fought to keep him away from Coulthard, whom he accused of causing the accident.

'Are you trying to kill me?' shouted Schumacher as he was dragged away from the McLaren pits. Schumacher was called to the stewards immediately after the race to account for his unruly behaviour, while Coulthard's car – which had lost its rear wing in the impact – was duly repaired and resumed the race to finish a distant seventh.

The stewards duly considered the incident and eventually dismissed it as a racing accident; no sanction was taken against either driver.

Coulthard refused to be intimidated by Schumacher's histrionics.

'Coming into the pits and asking me whether I was trying to kill him is totally unacceptable,' he said. 'I can't find words to describe how disappointed I am in Michael as a man that he could still be in that state after driving back to the pits.

'It was disgusting behaviour. If he still feels the same when he has calmed down, I have no further interest in discussing the matter with him.'

Hill had led the restarted race until lap nine, when Schumacher outbraked him neatly into the tight chicane just before the pits. Thereafter the acknowledged Spa ace edged away from the Jordan, seemingly on course to take the World Championship lead for the first time this season with what would have been a fifth win on this circuit, matching the record established by Ayrton Senna. Schumacher kept his lead through a single refuelling stop at the end of lap 16 when his Goodyear intermediate tyres were changed for full wets as the rain intensified. Hill came in on the same lap and resumed 22 seconds behind the Ferrari, an advantage which Schumacher extended to 37.7 seconds before colliding with Coulthard.

Quite why Schumacher was pushing on so audaciously in such terrible conditions when he had such a huge advantage and could hardly fail to take the Championship lead at the end of the day remained a mystery. What was even more remarkable was that the Ferrari driver was scheduled to make a second routine refuelling stop next time round.

This drama now left Hill ahead of his team-mate Ralf Schumacher running first and second at the head of the field in their Jordans. The young German driver is no respecter of reputations and was clearly anxious to score the first F1 win of his own short career, closing slightly on Hill as the race went into its closing stages.

With Jean Alesi's Sauber coming up hard in third place, both Jordan drivers knew they had to press on as hard as possible, but with eight laps to go the team manager told Schumacher over the radio that he should hold second place and not challenge Hill any further.

There must have been times over the previous two seasons since leaving Williams that Hill wondered whether he would ever win again. Now he was buoyant and upbeat, determined to build on this win to achieve more success for Jordan.

'I think we can be strong at Monza,' he predicted, 'but for now I just want to go out and celebrate this win.'

In the run-up to the Italian Grand Prix, Ferrari raised the temperature of its rivalry with McLaren by again blaming David Coulthard for the Spa accident. The Italian team's news release seemed provocatively timed to coincide with Coulthard's appearance at Monza for testing in preparation for Ferrari's home race ten days later. As the Scot accelerated out on to the circuit he was greeted with cat-calls and shouts of disapproval from the crowd.

The release from the Italian team claimed that

After some disconcerting interpretations, Ferrari has once again examined all the various film and photographic evidence from the race, which shows unequivocally that, for almost an entire lap, Coulthard ignored the blue flags and never allowed Schumacher to go by; on several occasions Schumacher moved off line to show Coulthard he was there and [that] Coulthard's sudden slowing down while on the racing line made the collision inevitable, given the poor visibility.

The bulletin made no mention of Schumacher's aggressive approach to Coulthard in the pit lane after the race, where he had to be restrained from approaching the Scottish driver.

'His [Schumacher's] actions were not those of a former champion,' said Clay Regazzoni, the former Ferrari driver who won the 1970 Italian Grand Prix. 'Michael is the best driver, but he knows it so well that he drives with arrogance and thinks he's a demi-God.'

McLaren issued a measured rebuttal of the Ferrari allegations, noting that it was 'understandable that immediately following this incident, emotions were running high and incorrect conclusions reached'. They also pointed out that the stewards had not blamed Coulthard and that examination of performance data downloaded from the McLaren's computer systems indicated that the driver did not do anything wrong.

It seemed clear there was little prospect of reconciling these two strong and opposing views, but McLaren diplomatically left the door open for a truce by stating that although 'it does not wish to become involved in a protracted public discussion with Ferrari on the incident, it extends an invitation to discuss the matter further in private if there is a wish to do so.'

Since Ferrari was apparently taking little notice of a pre-season pact between its President Luca di Montezemolo and McLaren Managing Director Ron Dennis to discuss any differences in private and not leak them to the press, the Italian team seemed unlikely to avail itself of such an offer.

As if to rub in the point, Schumacher then set up the World Championship for a dramatic grandstand finish by producing the precious victory which 125,000 car-crazy Monza race fans had dreamed of, yet could hardly bring themselves to believe seriously possible.

Even after Schumacher had secured his first pole position of the 1998 season here on Ferrari's home ground, events seemed to surrender to the worst fears of the crowd as the McLaren–Mercedes of championship leader Mika Häkkinen and his team-mate David Coulthard catapulted through from the second row of the grid to take an immediate first and second places.

'My start was terrible,' said Schumacher afterwards. 'I got everything wrong which I could have got wrong. I was lucky to catch up Jacques [Villeneuve] in the second corner to get back behind Eddie and obviously he let me by, which enabled me to catch up the McLarens. I wasn't expecting that, to be honest.'

Yet with Coulthard suffering an engine failure and Häkkinen limping home fourth after a lurid spin caused by sudden brake problems, it all turned out fine at the end of the day. Schumacher surged home to score the second Ferrari 1–2 of the season, with Eddie Irvine finishing 37 seconds behind. Just to add to the family celebrations, the two Ferrari drivers were joined on the podium by Michael's younger brother Ralf, who finished a strong third in the Jordan–Honda.

'After our poor performance at Hockenheim, which is also a low downforce circuit, we thought that Monza would be very difficult for us,' said Michael. 'But all the hard work paid off today. Now I am looking forward to the Nürburgring and Suzuka, as both circuits should suit our car.'

The Ferrari team leader now went into the penultimate round of the title chase, the Luxembourg Grand Prix, tied on 80 points with Häkkinen, and facing his home crowd at the Nürburgring with a distinct sense of optimism. Yet Häkkinen again turned the McLaren–Mercedes fortunes around to produce a brilliant victory which ensured a spine-tingling finale to the season at Suzuka.

Häkkinen led by just four points. Michael had to win with Mika no higher than third in Japan, so the pressure was firmly on Eddie Irvine to help. In the event, Michael blitzed his way to pole position only to stall at the start and have to take what was in fact the second restart from the back of the grid. Häkkinen won easily and it was all over.

The F1 rules are unequivocal about procedure on the grid. If you stall and cause the race to be restarted, you go to the back of the class. At the first start, Jarno Trulli's Prost was the culprit. The start was aborted and the hapless Italian had to take his medicine. Then Michael stalled at the second start and there was no preferential treatment for the twice World Champion. It was a disastrous setback for the Ferrari ace, possibly attributable to the fact that he had already given his F300's clutch mechanism a touch too much punishment with a couple of dummy starts prior to arriving on the final grid. These F1 clutches are delicate components and can easily go out of their super-fine adjustment.

The moment he selected first gear, the clutch may have dragged momentarily, causing the V10 engine to stall. Perhaps the strain was getting to him. More likely the hydraulics overheated and the clutch sensors became scrambled. Either way, it effectively wiped Michael out as a World Championship contender.

Yet he would not give up without a fight. From 21st and last on the grid, Ferrari number three was through to 13th place mid-way round the opening lap once the race got under way. By the end of that lap he was 12th, then tenth on lap two, ninth on lap three and eighth behind brother Ralf's Jordan on lap four. Ralf didn't make it difficult for him to slip by, but then he latched on to the tail of a ferocious chase behind Damon Hill's Jordan which was tailing Jacques Villeneuve's Williams and David Coulthard's fourth-placed McLaren. David had got too much wheelspin at the start and found himself boxed in behind Heinz-Harald Frentzen's Williams from the word go. And none of this group was particularly interested in conceding any ground to Schumacher's Ferrari.

From his lowly starting position, Schumacher drove brilliantly to climb to third before his right rear tyre failed following a deflation almost certainly caused by running over debris from a spectacular collision between Toranosuke Takagi's Tyrrell and Esteban Tuero's Minardi at the chicane before the pits.

The tyre failed on the 165 mph plunge towards the first right-hander, but Michael controlled the wayward Ferrari with characteristic brilliance. He pulled up and parked on the side of the track, his day done. Schumacher had experienced a front wheel vibration for three laps prior to this disaster, having flat-spotted the front Goodyear under braking for the chicane.

'Mika and his team deserved the title,' said Schumacher reflectively after the race. 'I think we did not lose the championship today at Suzuka, but in the early part of the season when we were too far behind. I do not feel too disappointed because I think Ferrari can be proud of what we achieved this season.'

Yet again, Michael had proved himself to be suffused with dazzling talent, an almost magical touch, behind the wheel. Yet, like the late Ayrton Senna whose mantle he had now assumed, he displayed an arrogance and intolerance of others. When he bundled Heinz-Harald Frentzen's Williams off the road at Montreal, he could scarcely bring himself to make a grudging apology. After hitting the back of David Coulthard's McLaren in the rain at Spa, he completely lost control of his temper. Yet the driving genius still transcended his weak and vulnerable points.

Michael himself offered the most straightforward explanation of his own success. In his view, he has a mental margin, not needing to use all his brain power in the heat of Grand Prix battle. Obviously he has all the outstanding balance, coordination and natural talent which are needed to be a top driver, but he was not a man who lay awake trying to analyse why he exerted such superiority over his frustrated rivals.

'Look, the ability I have is a natural thing,' he explains. 'I don't work at it, and I don't have to make big preparations before I get into the car.

'I just do up the straps, start the engine, let in the clutch – and do what I do.' All the other drivers must find themselves wishing it was all so blindingly straightforward.

Chapter Six

Championship lost

It was a graphic reminder of the millions of pounds involved in contemporary Grand Prix racing that when Michael Schumacher traded up to a sleek Challenger private jet in 1998, his manager Willi Weber purchased the smaller used Cessna Citation plane which the Ferrari ace was discarding. It was a deal which raised the prospect of the F1 manager now being rich enough to need his own manager. Yet if Weber, a sleek suited, well-coiffed Stuttgart-based entrepreneur, can afford his own wings, then he has certainly earned the privilege. Take Schumacher's genius at the wheel out of the equation and it was 54-year-old Weber who had almost singlehandedly been responsible for the German driver's rise to fame and fortune.

At home in Germany, Michael continued to ride on a tidal wave of popular support probably transcending even similarly public displays of adulation towards fellow German sporting legends such as Boris Becker and Jürgen Klinsmann. By the end of the 1998 season the Ferrari driver, still only 29 years of age, had amassed no fewer than 33 Grand Prix victories. That put him eight away from Ayrton Senna's tally of 41 and a more challenging 18 away from Alain Prost's all-time record.

Even the controversy at Jeréz in 1997, where he rammed his Ferrari into the side of Jacques Villeneuve's overtaking Williams in an effort to settle the outcome of the World

Championship, had failed materially to dent his popularity. There were short-term criticisms, sure; but Schumacher quickly regained his status in the eyes of the fans. The so-called punishment of disqualification from second place in that year's World Championship brought with it an obligation for him to help with a European road safety campaign backed by motor racing's governing body, the FIA. This exercise was deftly turned into something of a PR triumph for the Ferrari driver.

There continued to be something compellingly attractive about the Little Boy Lost demeanour of this lad from the wrong side of the tracks who has made the Big Time. Schumacher himself continued to trust Weber's judgement completely. 'If they have a new sponsor of a contract, Willi will do all the negotiations,' said a Schumacher camp insider. 'If the terms seem to Willi's liking, he will then present them to Michael.

'This is a serious partnership; they are business colleagues and close friends. Willi knows that his main priority is to take all the worries off Michael's shoulders. It is very important that he has his mind free for what he does best, the racing.'

Such a division of labour clearly worked well. At the same time Weber's assiduous dealings should ensure that his driver earns around $125 million from retainers and marketing agreements under the terms of his latest Ferrari contract, which lasts through to the end of 2002. Less Weber's commission, of course, which is put at around 20 per cent.

Ironically, it seemed increasingly unlikely that the German ace would ever drive a Mercedes-engined car in Formula One. At a Mercedes shareholders' meeting in the summer of 1998, board director Jürgen Schrempp emphasized that the car company wanted Mika Häkkinen and David Coulthard to continue driving the McLarens which are powered by its engines.

Mercedes insiders hinted that Schumacher carried with him a little too much controversial baggage: the collision with Damon Hill which resolved the 1994 World Championship, the incident with Villeneuve at Jeréz . . . By contrast, Ferrari wanted the very best driver available and was prepared to put up with everything to keep him.

Under such circumstances, it was quite understandable that Ferrari accepted Michael's requirement that they sign an acquiescent number two driver who was prepared to play second fiddle. That said, Irvine proved to be a solid team player who admitted that only occasionally did he feel he could match Schumacher's absolute speed.

At the start of the 1999 season it was almost twenty years since Jody Scheckter had last clinched the drivers' World Championship at the wheel of a Ferrari, leading his team-mate Gilles Villeneuve – father of Jacques – across the line at Monza to win the 1979 Italian Grand Prix.

Team orders played a part in the outcome of that particular race, but in a subtly different manner. In those days, Ferrari standing orders required that the team's cars should not race each other once they had assumed first and second places at the head of the field. Villeneuve abided by those rules that day, only to be double-crossed three years later when Didier Pironi tricked him on the last lap of the '82 San Marino Grand Prix at Imola and sneaked through to win. Two weeks later, Jacques Villeneuve's father was killed at Zolder, probably trying to beat Pironi's quicker lap time in qualifying for the Belgian Grand Prix.

In 1961, Germany's Wolfgang von Trips had stood poised to clinch the World Championship only to be killed, along with more than a dozen spectators, when he crashed in the Italian Grand Prix. His team-mate Phil Hill won the title, but believes pressure of intra-team rivalry almost certainly contributed to von Trips's crash.

In those days, of course, the team owners called the shots. Enzo Ferrari bestrode the Grand Prix world like an irascible automotive Colossus, paying his star drivers a few hundred dollars a month and invariably heightening the tension among them by failing to nominate a team leader. In the era of Michael Schumacher, the terms at Ferrari were dictated by the best driver in the world. He knew just how difficult it really is to win a World Championship and did not intend to let the interests of his team-mate get in the way of his own towering ambition.

At the start of the 1999 season Ferrari switched to Bridgestone rubber, along with the rest of the field, after Goodyear finally withdrew from the F1 business and left its Japanese rival with a monopoly supply situation. The latest Ferrari F399 was an evolutionary version of the previous year's car, and Schumacher began the season in a mood of measured optimism about its prospects. Yet in the pubs and clubs in downtown Melbourne through the night after the Australian Grand Prix it was Eddie Irvine they were celebrating, after Schumacher's team-mate had saved the day for Ferrari in the opening round of the 1999 title chase. The 32-year-old had picked up the fallen standard for Maranello to score his own personal maiden F1 victory – a feat that certainly seemed to cause the rest of the paddock more than a passing degree of wry amusement.

Maranello's dutiful number two was handed this golden opportunity at his 82nd attempt after both the McLaren–Mercedes of Mika Häkkinen and David Coulthard wilted with technical problems. On this occasion, Schumacher found himself forced into a nightmare repeat of his Suzuka '98 scenario, being relegated to the back of the grid after a clutch problem just prior to yet another F1 restart. It made you wonder just what Michael had to do to appease the gods.

Irvine won superbly by just a second from Heinz-Harald Frentzen, the former Williams driver having a fine debut outing for Jordan on a day which saw his team-mate Damon Hill spinning into a gravel trap on the opening lap. Ralf Schumacher celebrated his switch to Williams with third place ahead of Giancarlo Fisichella's Benetton, rounding off a popular and much-acclaimed result for F1's emergent generation.

'It was good that Michael did so much testing for me,' grinned Eddie, obliquely referring to Schumacher's intense winter programme. 'He did the sweating and I got the glory.

'From the start of practice on Friday I was convinced that if I could get the softer tyre choice to work I could do well. Heinz was pushing me hard but I pressed like hell after the safety car came out [for the second time, after Alex Zanardi crashed his Williams] and pulled out two seconds to keep ahead of him at the fuel stop.'

Irvine then went off to Brazil determined to hang on to his title points lead and go to Imola ahead of the pursuing pack. But Michael was not about to let another opportunity slip through his fingers. He got his programme firmly back on track with a fine second place at Interlagos, the challenging track on the fringes of the country's second city, São Paolo. Michael reported that the car felt good during the race. But Häkkinen in the McLaren–Mercedes recovered from an early gear-change problem to take the initiative, and won after a tactically astute performance – but Michael certainly served notice that he was firmly back on track and in contention.

It was a good day for Ferrari, even though both F399s were outgunned in terms of sheer power. Eddie Irvine tracked Ralf Schumacher's Williams home to take fifth place, despite an unscheduled late race stop to top up the air bottle for the V10 engine's pneumatic valve-gear mechanism. That meant he would go into the San Marino Grand Prix leading the World Championship – which guaranteed him hero status in Italy for the following three weeks!

At Imola, however, it was a combination of Michael Schumacher's flair in traffic and Ross Brawn's shrewd strategic management from the pit wall which delivered a decisive victory over a demoralized Coulthard. Michael led the McLaren past the chequered flag by just four seconds for the 34th win of his career, which vaulted him into the lead of the drivers' World Championship after only three races. He played it cool in the opening stages, then made his first refuelling stop on lap 31 while Coulthard stayed out for another four laps.

Taking into account the two drivers' refuelling stops, Schumacher made up a crucial seven seconds on Coulthard during this period of the race. It saw him get ahead of the McLaren driver when Coulthard made his sole refuelling stop, after which the Ferrari team leader was able to open up a 21.8-second lead which saw him through his second 'splash and dash' refuelling stop without relinquishing his advantage.

Schumacher had originally moved up to second place behind Coulthard when Mika Häkkinen made a rare error and crashed out of the race on lap 17.

'It is very unusual for either of our drivers to make mistakes,' said Ron Dennis, 'but Mika made one today – better now than at the end of last year. David's chance to win the race was taken away by the behaviour of several backmarkers and I am disappointed in the lack of sporting behaviour from their team managers.'

That was all very well, but Schumacher rammed home his advantage in a super-fast 15-lap middle stint of the race leading up to his second refuelling stop. A succession of laps in the 1-minute 28-second bracket left him with a virtually bullet-proof advantage.

Unfortunately, Eddie Irvine was not around at the finish to consolidate his third place, the other Ferrari having dropped out 15 laps before the finish to go with engine failure, when apparently set for a place on the podium.

McLaren's embarrassment continued at Monaco, where Michael won again. With his pole position McLaren–Mercedes brimful of fuel for a one-stop race with a particularly long opening stint, the Finn knew he had to make it to the first corner if he was to have any prospect of winning. Schumacher gave him no chance, and as the F399 sailed through to complete the opening lap of the 78-lap race already 1.3 seconds ahead of his key rival, one sensed that the race's outcome was already beyond doubt.

Thereafter the German ace delivered a copybook performance to clinch Ferrari's first 1–2 finish ahead of Eddie Irvine on this, the most glitzy and glamorous venue on the F1 calendar.

It was Michael's 35th career win – putting him only six behind the late Ayrton Senna's total – and earned him the accolade of most successful Ferrari F1 driver of all time with 16 wins, one ahead of Niki Lauda. Quite an achievement.

This awesome performance from Schumacher sprang in part from his F399's perfectly balanced chassis extracting the maximum performance from his choice of hard compound Bridgestone tyres. With Bridgestone introducing a new extra-soft compound, tyre choice was clearly going to be more than usually critical from the outset. With the addition of a fourth groove on the front tyres this season, the abiding tendency towards understeer had been aggravated. That is the last characteristic a driver needs at Monaco, so the decision which had to be made was whether it was worth trading the extra grip of the softer compound for the better handling balance of the harder rubber.

Schumacher's Ferrari was certainly nice to drive. 'Up to my refuelling stop I was pushing hard to build up my advantage,' he said, 'and after the stop I just drove it home.

'There was not so much flexibility within my own race strategy but I made sure that the gap never dropped below 20 seconds. I squeezed ahead of Mika going into the first corner which, to be honest, made it all much easier from the start.'

Häkkinen bounced back to win the Spanish Grand Prix at Barcelona, Michael finishing a distant third after spending the opening phase of the chase bottled up behind Jacques Villeneuve's fast-starting British American 01.

Mika then made it two in a row when a rare driving error on Schumacher's part dropped a Canadian Grand Prix victory into his lap, moving the McLaren–Mercedes driver into a championship lead for the first time that season.

Make no mistake about it, from the moment Schumacher's pole position Ferrari F399 ruthlessly – and very rudely – chopped across Häkkinen's McLaren to protect his lead in the opening seconds of the race, the two top title protagonists were at it hammer and tongs. Trading fastest laps as if they were in the final moments of qualifying, the two rivals quickly left the opposition in their dust.

On lap 30 came what some would later remember as the defining moment of the season. Coming through the fast right/left S-bend before the start line, Schumacher suddenly lost front-end grip. The Ferrari lurched into an understeering twitch and there simply wasn't room for Michael to catch it again. He slammed into the wall and out of the race.

He was in good company. Former World Champions Damon Hill and Jacques Villeneuve parked their Jordan and BAR respectively in the concrete at the same point. Several others came close and got away with it by the skin of their wheel rims.

'It was very dusty at that point of the circuit,' shrugged Schumacher. 'I reckon to make one big mistake a year and I guess this was it. It was clearly my mistake and I apologize to the team.'

From that point onwards, Häkkinen had the race to himself. Through a single routine scheduled refuelling stop, the Finn never had a moment's worry. He ran across the grass briefly at the S-bend before the pits, but otherwise he was in control all the way.

Häkkinen's second place to Heinz-Harald Frentzen's Jordan in the rain-soaked French Grand Prix strengthened his points tally to 40, eight ahead of Michael Schumacher whose Ferrari finished fifth, dutifully tailed home by his team-mate Eddie Irvine, who certainly seemed much quicker in the closing stages but is contractually debarred from overtaking his more exalted colleague.

'Everything that could go wrong did go wrong today,' said Irvine. 'I was in neutral at the start and lost time as I had to select first again. I knew it was going to rain, so I decided to take it carefully at first.

'When the rain came I radioed the pits. I thought they might not be 100 per cent ready and it was a bad stop, and without it I might have finished higher.'

In fact the Ferrari mechanics mistakenly began to fit another set of dry weather tyres before realizing their error and putting on another set of wet tyres. As a result a stop which should have taken around nine seconds took a shambolic 42.9, effectively writing the Ulsterman out of the competition.

This was bitterly disappointing for Irvine, who otherwise could have just squeezed through into the lead when the bulk of the front runners made their first stop in heavy rain next time round. In fact, Ferrari's slip might well have cost him a race victory.

A fortnight later, Irvine chased Coulthard home for first and second places in the British Grand Prix at Silverstone. But even before that battle was resolved, the race had already gone down in the history books as one of the key turning points in recent F1 history.

It was the day when Michael Schumacher's Ferrari plunged off the road in a 190 mph accident which left him with serious leg injuries and Mika Häkkinen's McLaren was prudently withdrawn from the battle after shedding its left rear wheel, leaving the number two drivers in both teams to pick up the gauntlet and produce a close-fought battle all the way to the chequered flag.

The long-term implications for the 1999 World Championship seemed immense. With Schumacher probably sidelined for at least a couple of months – and five or six races – he looked effectively a spent force as far as the quest for Ferrari's first drivers' title since 1979 was concerned. Häkkinen's second title crown now seemed little more than a formality.

Nevertheless, on a day inevitably clouded by the sombre sight of Ferrari's brilliant team leader clattering away to hospital in a medical helicopter, Coulthard's win represented a crucial moment of restoration for the easy-going 28-year-old who had last tasted the victory champagne in the previous year's San Marino Grand Prix.

Schumacher's nightmare began in the first few yards of the race when the advantage of his second-row starting position immediately slipped away as Häkkinen and Coulthard ripped their McLarens into first and second places. As if to add insult to injury, Eddie Irvine's Ferrari surged majestically round the outside of the German ace going into Copse, pushing him back to fourth.

Down through the nightmarishly quick S-bend at Becketts, Schumacher came hard at Irvine and slipstreamed on to his tail as the two Ferraris accelerated hard up to 185 mph. Irvine glanced in his mirror and dutifully allowed Schumacher just enough room for a free passage down the inside into the tricky Stowe right-hander which tightens up on itself as it leads round into the Vale.

Suddenly everything went wrong. Instead of cutting a gentle arc to the right, Michael locked up his front brakes.

From then on everything was lost. The Ferrari skidded on to the gravel trap – which did virtually nothing in terms of reducing his speed – and slammed head-on into the retaining tyre wall.

The horrifying impact ripped off the front end of the Ferrari monocoque. Schumacher caught his breath and began to lift himself from the shattered car. After a moment's effort, he slumped back into the cockpit as marshals swarmed round the vehicle. He had sustained a double fracture below his right knee and would have to wait for the ambulance to arrive before being released from the wreckage. Extricated, he was taken off to the circuit medical centre, jauntily waving to his fans from the stretcher.

Ironically, at the point Schumacher lost control the race had already been red-flagged to a halt as Jacques Villeneuve's British American 01 and Alex Zanardi's Williams had stalled on the starting grid. The McLaren pit radioed to both Häkkinen and Coulthard that this was the case, but Irvine explained that he had heard nothing from his pit. One must assume it was the same for Schumacher.

'I had to touch the brakes to avoid David [Coulthard] going into Becketts on the first lap and it's possible that Michael may have touched me and damaged his front wing,' said Irvine. 'All I know is that he came flying past me all locked up. I think he just outbraked himself.'

On the face of it, this seemed the logical view. Schumacher had been frustrated by the handling of his car during the race morning warm-up and made a quick fix change to the set-up in an effort to improve things. He was then jumped into Copse by Irvine and might just have been willing to take one risk too many as he slammed into Stowe in a bad mood.

However, having examined all the technical data at their disposal, the Ferrari team concluded that a rear brake malfunction had caused the accident.

Häkkinen had been ahead at the first start and then duplicated that performance when the race got under way for a second time 40 minutes later. The Finn confidently pulled away from Irvine and Coulthard in the opening stages, only to lose the lead half a lap after his first refuelling stop on lap 26 when a left rear wheel worked loose. This was replaced, tightened – and then flew off the car coming onto the start/finish straight, but he managed to three-wheel back to the pits for repairs. Resuming last, he began to climb back through the field when McLaren called him in to retire on precautionary grounds. That left the path open for Coulthard to vault ahead of Irvine at his second refuelling stop and control the race to the finish.

Schumacher's accident happened at probably the worst place on the Silverstone circuit at which to suffer any sort of brake failure. Once he left the tarmac, trying desperately to brake at around 160 mph, there was absolutely nothing he could do but hang on grimly. Had he suffered the same failure at any one of a number of other points on the circuit – say the Bridge, Priory, Brooklands or Luffield corners – he would in all probability have spun to a halt in a cloud of tyre smoke, undone his belt and walked away. It was just the wrong place for the wrong type of failure.

Detailed examination of the Ferrari computer read-outs confirmed to the team's engineers that the car had suffered a rear brake failure, but a routine check on Irvine's car produced no cause for concern and there were no worries about allowing him to take the restart.

Schumacher's escape with relatively minor injuries was certainly a relief for the Ferrari personnel, although they were also understandably dejected faced with the depressing prospect that their much-heralded F1 renaissance had stalled in the pits for the third successive season.

It was six years since Jean Todt, the highly regarded former Peugeot competitions manager, had been recruited by Ferrari as Sporting Director, charged with rebuilding the team to the point where it could again win a World Championship. Now the deadline for another title crown had come and gone, and it looked as if Schumacher's injuries might cause those ambitions to be deferred once again to the 2000 season.

Some F1 insiders naturally began to question whether the Ferrari team would be able to sustain their massive emotional intensity of effort after three such huge disappointments. Moreover, at just the time they needed to put their whole weight behind Eddie Irvine's thrust for the championship, some remarks from Todt struck a distinctly discordant note, questioning whether the Ulsterman's temperament might prevent him from taking a tilt at the title.

'The championship will be tough to win for us,' he said. 'But we will give it everything and only time will tell what will happen. I hope Irvine can win the drivers' title. Life has been such that he has often been behind Michael, but Michael will not be there for a few weeks, so it's up to him to win as much as he can.

'He has never been the second driver. It is the facts which have decided that Irvine is the second driver because Michael has always been faster than him. If he had been ahead of Michael then he would have been the first driver.'

This certainly did not quite square with the frequently admitted fact that Irvine's contract specifically required him to defer to Schumacher on all occasions, stay behind the German driver and allow him past if necessary.

As for Irvine himself, he believed he could close the eight-point deficit to Mika Häkkinen and make a serious bid for the championship. He realized that over-shooting at his first refuelling stop at Silverstone had in fact probably cost him victory over David Coulthard's McLaren.

'I've just got to take it race by race,' said Irvine, 'but people can be assured that I will give it my all for the championship. This is not exactly the way I wanted to be a number one, though. The team needs Michael back because we've got a Constructors' Championship to win as well.'

One man who knew all about the challenge of recovering from a serious accident was Mika Häkkinen. He recalled graphically the first test drive he took at the Paul Ricard circuit after recovering from his 150 mph accident in practice for the 1995 Australian Grand Prix.

'If my accident had been due to a mistake of mine, I don't think I would have come back to F1,' he said. 'The first day of the test was really weird. Was I going to like it or wasn't I? Then when I started driving really fast I started looking around me and thinking "Jesus, if I go off there . . ." But it didn't slow me down.'

Schumacher would not have to wrestle with the issue of what caused his accident. 'The results from the telemetry are very clear,' said Ferrari spokesman Claudio Berro. 'The braking on the rear wheels [of Schumacher's car] was zero. All this talk about steering and throttle problems is just not right. The result is clear, but now we have to find the precise cause.'

That was a relief, sure enough. But given that another stab at the championship was surely lost, would the German's legendary motivation and focus finally begin to waver? Lying trapped in the wreckage of his Ferrari on Saturday afternoon, he could have been forgiven for wondering whether he really needed to live his life on such a precarious knife-edge any longer. He was massively wealthy, with a fortune reputed to be in excess of £100 million. He had won 35 Grands Prix and two World Championships, yet seemed as far as ever from taking a third. He had a young family and a contract with Ferrari which would see him take over the role of sporting ambassador when he finally retired. Perhaps he would choose to advance those plans?

No: Michael Schumacher was made of much more resilient, sterner stuff. From his hospital bed in Northampton he vowed he would be back in the cockpit of his Ferrari before the end of the season.

'I know I'm going to be out of action for two to three months and I realize that I've absolutely no chance of the championship this year,' he said. 'But I'm confident that I'll be back driving a Ferrari in F1 before the end of the season.'

Schumacher underwent a 90-minute operation on his right leg which was fractured below the knee. Surgeon Bill Ribbans revealed that the operation was a complete success, with just one pin needed to hold the bones in place, both of which had sustained a clean break.

After spending two nights in hospital, Schumacher was flown home to a clinic near his home in Switzerland. He admitted that he was lucky to be alive after the accident.

'I am thankful for the improvements made in he cars over the last few years,' he said, 'because that is what helped me escape with only a broken leg. It was a very scary moment, because it was the first time it has ever happened to me. At first I could not get out of the car and I was worried about the situation.'

As Michael's injuries slowly healed, so Irvine did his best for himself and the Ferrari team. He did very well, in fact, winning both the Austrian and German Grands Prix in fine style to emerge as a credible title challenger in his own right.

As things turned out, Schumacher was a little too anxious to force the pace of his recovery. By the end of August he was back in a Ferrari testing at Mugello and then overdid things with a spell of mountain biking in southern France. Not even the German driver's huge determination could artificially accelerate nature's healing process.

However, by the end of September he was ready to go and, on 8 October 1999, dropped a bombshell when he announced that he would, after all, be competing in the last two Grands Prix of the season in Malaysia and Japan. The news dramatically strengthened his Ferrari team-mate Eddie Irvine's challenge for the championship, as Schumacher was expected to offer crucial tactical support to the Ulsterman.

Irvine was currently just two points behind McLaren–Mercedes team leader Mika Häkkinen with just those two races to go, and the news that Schumacher would be back in action inevitably intensified the pressure on the Finn after a disappointing season punctuated by accidents, mechanical failures and driving errors.

McLaren now faced little choice but to instruct David Coulthard, currently fourth in the championship, to provide Häkkinen with as much tactical assistance as Schumacher would afford Irvine, adding an intriguing element of unpredictability and tension to the last two rounds of the title chase.

Schumacher's presence would also enable Ferrari to make a credible bid for the Constructors' Championship, in which they trailed McLaren by eight points prior to the Malaysian race.

The German driver's announcement to return came at the end of a week of apparent indecision. Initially Schumacher had felt that, despite being given a positive medical assessment by a specialist Dr Gerard Sailient in Paris, he lacked the stamina to survive through a 200-mile Grand Prix. However, after setting competitive testing times in the Ferrari F399 at both Mugello and Fiorano, he finally announced that he would, after all, be back in the cockpit in Malaysia – just 14 weeks after his accident.

'After three days of intensive testing, Michael saw that there had been a big improvement in his physical condition,' said a Ferrari spokesman. 'Therefore he has decided to take part in the two final and very important races of the season, to give the maximum support to Ferrari in the fight for the championships and to fulfil the wishes of the team and all the fans.'

When he arrived at Kuala Lumpur's lavish new Sepang circuit, Michael kept the opposition guessing. Initially he hinted that Irvine might be battling alone against Häkkinen and might not be receiving any additional assistance from him.

'I have heard it said that I have been made to drive,' said Schumacher after his arrival from Europe, 'but I am independent enough to make by own decisions.

'The team asked me to test things on the car [last week] and, although I said I could manage only five laps at a time, this was a lucky moment for me because I felt comfortable [in the car].

'I am first of all driving here for the team and not in the interests of Eddie Irvine. I can help him by being in front and then letting him by, but if that is not the case, he will have to manage on his own.

'I feel I can win the race because I feel fresh, but it will certainly be difficult as I do not feel I can go flat out yet from the first lap to the last.'

It was crystal clear from Schumacher's remarks that the main focus of his efforts would be to help Ferrari win its first Constructors' World Championship since 1983. All the same, it was hard to avoid concluding that Schumacher still wanted to be Ferrari's first World Champion since 1979 and, to this end, had little interest in supporting Irvine's title bid, only to see him take the coveted title-holder's race number one over to the newly branded Jaguar team, which he was to join at the start of 2000.

There were also many on the inside of the sport expressing concern that Schumacher had hurried his physical recovery with excessive zeal and was showing undue haste in this bid to return to the cockpit of a Grand Prix car. Also, despite its denials, it seemed that the Ferrari senior management was privately concerned that Schumacher – in initially talking down his chances of returning for the final two races – was playing a political game. Either he was quick enough to race, or he should not have climbed into the cockpit of an F1 car in the first place. If he was good enough to test at competitive speeds, then surely he was fit enough to race. That seemed now to be the lesson that Michael had taken aboard!

Come the race, Michael Schumacher effectively won the Grand Prix for Irvine in a brilliantly orchestrated demonstration of team tactics which seemed to leave the Ulsterman a firm favourite to clinch the World Championship in the final round of the series at Suzuka two weeks later. Yet less than two hours after the end of the race the paddock was rocked with a technical bombshell when FIA F1 technical delegate Jo Bauer submitted a report to the stewards of the meeting saying that, in his view, the two Ferrari F399s did not conform with the technical regulations.

His report stated that, when checking the bodywork facing the ground, it was noticed that parts of the deflector panels 'did not lie on either the reference or step planes' in accordance with the F1 technical regulations. The rules required that the flat bottom of the car – between the front and rear wheels – should effectively 'mirror' all the appendages on the chassis. Therefore the undertray profile should have covered the entire aerodynamic deflectors – or 'barge boards' – which, in the Ferraris' case, they did not.

FIA technical delegate Jo Bauer submitted this information to the three independent stewards, in this case Irishman Bryan Brophy, South Africa's Derek Ledger and Malaysia's Dr K. Kanagalingam. They took less than an hour to decide that the Ferraris had indeed infringed the rules and therefore had to be disqualified from the race subject to appeal. This meant promoting Mika Häkkinen's third-placed McLaren–Mercedes to take the win ahead of the Stewart–Fords of Johnny Herbert and Rubens Barrichello.

Ferrari sporting director Jean Todt later confirmed that the team would lodge an appeal. 'The cars were inspected both here and at the last race at the Nürburgring and were found to be OK,' he stated.

At the start of the race Schumacher had surged into an immediate lead, opening a 3.1-second advantage by the end of the second lap even though his Ferrari was running in heavier trim with a bigger fuel load for a one-stop race strategy. Having made the point that he was back in business with a vengeance, Schumacher then eased back and relinquished the lead to Irvine mid-way round lap four. A couple of corners later David Coulthard's McLaren–Mercedes came at his Ferrari in a rush and squeezed through into second place, a move which was certainly not part of the Ferrari game plan and saw the two cars make firm contact, slightly damaging Schumacher's front wing.

As Coulthard tore away in hot pursuit of Irvine's leading Ferrari, Schumacher eased back to keep Häkkinen from posing any sort of threat to his team-mate. Coulthard closed to within a second of Irvine and looked almost certain to get past, only for his outside chance of winning the World Championship to end with fuel pressure problems after 15 laps. Irvine was eight seconds ahead of Schumacher when he came in for his first refuelling stop on lap 24. He resumed fourth, but got back ahead of Häkkinen when the Finn made his first stop at the end of lap 27.

On lap 28 the remarkable Schumacher made his sole refuelling stop and squeezed back into the race second behind Irvine, resuming his forced restraint of Häkkinen who by now was getting extremely frustrated with the Ferrari driver.

In the closing stages of the race Schumacher found that his rear tyres were wearing so badly that his car was sliding around all over the track, so he was happy that Häkkinen's second stop dropped the McLaren driver well back in his rear-view mirrors – happy, at least, until the scrutineers cast their critical eye over the scarlet Italian cars.

Twice during the course of the 56-lap inaugural race on the magnificent new Sepang circuit Schumacher had gifted the lead to Irvine; and he had spent much of the afternoon keeping Häkkinen boxed up in third place all the way to the chequered flag.

'It was a fantastic result for me and Ferrari,' said Irvine who vaulted from two points behind Häkkinen to four points ahead going into the final race of the season. 'Michael did a fantastic job for me and I could not have won without him.'

On the face of it, the Ferrari squad had dramatically outmanoeuvred McLaren in terms of race tactics, and while Häkkinen was clearly deeply depressed that he had to settle for third place, he had no criticism of Ferrari's tactics.

'It was the hardest race of my life,' said the Finn, whose two-point championship advantage had just been transformed at a stroke into a four-point deficit. 'I was flat out all the way. Ferrari had brilliant tactics and I don't really blame them.'

For his part, Schumacher said he was delighted to have helped Irvine, effectively acknowledging all the assistance the Ulsterman had given him over the past three seasons.

'I do the same as I have expected people to do for me,' he said. 'I preferred to win the race, for sure, but it doesn't make any sense. I didn't want to score a glorious win and then have us lose the World Championship.

'Everything we did as far as race tactics are concerned was done within the rules. It is part of the business of the game.'

Six days later, a scrum of television vans, tangled electrical cables, satellite dishes and aerials crammed the Place de la Concorde in Paris outside the offices of the Automobile Club de France as the massed ranks of the world motorsporting media crammed into a second floor conference room in a mood of fevered anticipation. They had convened to hear FIA President Max Mosley, sandy-haired and sober-suited, announce that the FIA Court of Appeal had overturned the stewards' decision from the Malaysian Grand Prix and reinstated the Ferrari F399s of Eddie Irvine and Michael Schumacher to first and second places.

'Ferrari came here with an accurate jig to show that all the relevant dimensions of the barge boards on the car were within the permitted 5 mm tolerance,' he explained, going on to tell the assembled journalists that the International Court of Appeal had confirmed that the dimensions of the turning vane (barge board) was within that margin of tolerance, 'provided the vane was properly attached to the car'.

The court also stated that 'the 10 mm dimension referred to in the technical delegate's report resulted from a method of measurement which was not necessarily in strict conformity with the regulations,' and 'the measuring equipment available to the FIA scrutineers at the Malaysian Grand Prix was not sufficiently accurate to call into question Ferrari's statement that the turning vane was indeed properly attached to the car.'

Mosley added: 'On an F1 car there are a large number of dimensions which fall into two categories. There are those which are a maximum or a minimum, and those with specific dimensions.

'When you have a maximum dimension you cannot flout that by even the smallest amount, but if you have a simple dimension such as the flat bottom, you have a tolerance, and we are satisfied that the tolerance of the Ferrari barge boards fell into those tolerances, possibly by less than 1 mm, but nevertheless conformed.'

Irvine was delighted. 'Never once did I ever believe Ferrari would have done something illegal to gain an advantage,' he said. 'That doesn't mean I wasn't worried, mind you, because you never know what can happen. This is great news, although after Ferrari put its case to the Appeal Court yesterday I already felt confident we had proved our point.

'This is the best possible result for Ferrari, for me and for the sport of Formula One. We are now going to have a cracking final weekend in Suzuka, which is my all-time favourite race track.'

Ferrari President Luca di Montezemolo echoed those sentiments. 'Ferrari is very satisfied with the verdict which overthrows the Stewards' decision taken at the Malaysian Grand Prix and which recognizes the total conformity of our cars with the regulations,' he said. 'This verdict reaffirms the values of the sport which have inspired Ferrari over fifty years and restores to us and our fans the great victory achieved on the track, which confirms the quality of our work.

'We worked quietly in order to demonstrate to the Court in a professional and incontrovertible manner the fundamental truth which led to the decision which has put to right so many unjust interpretations levelled against us these past few days, about which I was very unhappy.

'Ferrari appreciates the seriousness and high level of professionalism with which the FIA Court of Appeal has dealt with this case. Now, all our energies are devoted to trying to win the final and decisive Japanese Grand Prix.

'The verdict of the FIA Court of Appeal completely absolves Ferrari, who will make no further comment, except to sincerely thank the Automobile Club d'Italia, for once again effectively defending Italian interests in the international arena.'

This was emphatically not a view shared by McLaren, whose official communiqué on the subject read: 'The West McLaren Mercedes team was invited to attend the International Court of Appeal hearing in Paris. In accepting the invitation, it was our understanding that there was an oral and written acceptance that there had been a breach of the Technical Regulations.

'In a case of a breach of the Technical Regulations during a race the penalty that has been consistently applied is the one that was given in Malaysia, namely that of exclusion.

'In the circumstances we felt that the decision of the Stewards was correct and consistent with the previous practices of F1. Our purpose in attending was to point out these and other matters, and to seek a consistent application of the rules as established in the past in similar circumstances.

'We were very surprised to learn the day before the hearing that Ferrari had decided to argue that they had, contrary to their previous admissions, not infringed the Technical Regulations at all.

'This argument was based on a submission that the FIA technical equipment and procedures were inadequate and an interpretation of the Technical Regulations in conflict with the previous accepted understanding within Formula One, including that of the FIA Race Director and FIA F1 Technical Delegate.'

At the end of the day, however, none of this mattered at all. In the final race of the season Häkkinen led from start to finish and retained his World Championship crown. For his part, Schumacher acknowledged that he had made a very bad start. 'I had a problem when I went off the grid on the parade lap and a similar problem during the race start,' he said. 'I went into wheelspin and made a mess of it.'

Mika's achievement made him only the seventh driver in the 50-year history of the World Championship to win back-to-back titles, a feat previously managed by Alberto Ascari, Juan Manuel Fangio, Jack Brabham, Alain Prost, Ayrton Senna and Michael Schumacher.

Meanwhile, second and third places for Michael Schumacher and Eddie Irvine were enough to win Ferrari its first Constructors' World Championship since 1983, even though the drivers' title eluded Irvine despite the additional boost given by the FIA Appeal Court's decision the previous week. Outclassed and outdriven, Irvine remained gracious in the extreme after being beaten into third place by the McLaren team leader and Michael Schumacher in the other Ferrari F399.

Schumacher, who had qualified brilliantly on pole position only to be beaten to the draw by Häkkinen, finished the race just 5.015 seconds behind the McLaren ace. The German driver was generous in his praise for Häkkinen's achievement, yet the manner in which he rounded on David Coulthard for holding him up half a lap in the middle of the race, costing him over three seconds, was vitriolic in the extreme.

'It was a different thing between me and Mika in Malaysia where I was actually racing for position and had not been lapped,' he said. 'In that position you can play tactics. But if you have been lapped, you should give space.

'David had passed many blue flags, and he had some kind of a problem, but he was really zig-zagging. Actually I am not sure now whether I should believe that what happened at Spa last year wasn't done purposely, the way he behaved today. The situation cost me, I think, about 10 seconds.'

In fact that was an exaggeration by seven seconds on the part of the German. For his part, Coulthard threatened to take legal action if Schumacher did not withdraw his allegations.

In some people's eyes, however, Schumacher had never quite managed to match up to his pole-winning supremacy in the race itself. Once he had been beaten off the line, he dropped away in the opening stages to such an extent that many people began to believe that either Mika was stopping three times – and therefore running with a light fuel load – or the Ferrari was stopping only once. In fact, both men ran two-stop strategies and Häkkinen took his rival apart, brilliantly and comprehensively.

The cynics, of course, had another field day, claiming that Michael really only wanted to help win the Constructors' Championship for Ferrari and was not too bothered about giving Irvine another leg-up towards the drivers' crown. In fact, Michael was clearly hell-bent on winning at Suzuka, obviously feeling he had done more than his fair share of charity work for Irvine a fortnight earlier in Malaysia.

The weekend had begun in a mood of frenzied anticipation, but the psychological advantage seemed subtly to shift from Irvine to Häkkinen as practice and qualifying unfolded. On Thursday, Eddie could be found wandering the walkway behind the pits, happy to shoot the breeze with anybody he bumped into.

David Coulthard set the ball rolling just 14 minutes into qualifying by setting a decent benchmark of 1 min 38.871 seconds; ten minutes later the dazzling scarlet Ferraris of

Schumacher and Eddie Irvine trickled down the pit lane in formation to start their bid for grid positions. Michael was right on the pace from the start. On his first flying lap he was a startling 0.7 seconds inside Coulthard's best at the first timing split, and he maintained that advantage right through to the end of the lap. It would have been even quicker had he not got into a slight twitch coming through the fast left-hander on to the return straight.

The Ferrari ace stopped the clocks at 1 minute 38.032 seconds, after which Häkkinen emerged from the pit and equalled his time to three places of decimals. This put everybody in mind of that amazing day at Jeréz two years earlier, where Jacques Villeneuve's Williams, Schumacher's Ferrari and Heinz-Harald Frentzen's Williams set identical times to take the first three places on the grid. This seemed to be F1 showmanship gone mad, even though a shrewd bookie would no doubt tell you that there was as much chance of a dead heat as the cars producing any other combination of time. Surely Bernie Ecclestone's presentational talents didn't extend to fiddling the timing mechanism? It was certainly a compelling thought, but hardly one which stood up to scrutiny.

Häkkinen, refreshed after a week's golfing in Indonesia with his wife Erja, had thrust aside the somewhat preoccupied demeanour which had clouded his efforts over the past three races. He seemed back on form, relaxed and more confident than ever. Just as he'd seemed 12 months earlier when he arrived to clinch his first world title.

Mika was set to counter-attack in a bid to regain oust Schumacher from pole position when he was floored by an accidental punch from an unexpected source. Trickling slowly through the pits chicane, trying to ensure plenty of track space ahead for a really quick lap, the Finn suddenly found Jean Alesi's Sauber bearing down on him at speed, the Frenchman hard at work on a quick lap.

Alesi lost downforce, straight-lined the chicane and reappeared on the circuit ahead of Häkkinen, immediately spinning, which forced Mika to do likewise. Each was extremely fed up with the other, but most observers agreed it was just one of those unfortunate things that happen in racing.

Coulthard played the tactical card on McLaren's behalf for some of the race, although he moved the wrong way at the start, allowing Irvine to get ahead of him on the run to the first corner. Eventually squeezing ahead of the Ulsterman's Ferrari as Eddie emerged from his first refuelling stop, Coulthard then tried to push him back into the clutches of Heinz-Harald Frentzen's Jordan and Ralf Schumacher's Williams. It didn't quite work, but Eddie lost 18 seconds in six laps before diving into the pits for an early second stop on lap 32. Then Coulthard, who had been grappling with gear-change problems caused by a hydraulic fluid leak, spun off and glanced a barrier. He got the car back to the pits for repairs, resumed, briefly held up Michael Schumacher and then quit for good as the gear-change problems worsened.

Heinz-Harald Frentzen finished a strong fourth in his Jordan 199, just squeezing out Ralf Schumacher's superbly driven Williams FW21 for a result which narrowly saved the Stewart team's fourth place in the title chase by a single point ahead of Williams.

If you were of a cynical disposition you might be tempted to conclude that Michael Schumacher was enjoying the post-race party after the Japanese Grand Prix just a little too much. He'd just finished second to Mika Häkkinen's McLaren and ahead of his Ferrari team-mate Eddie Irvine. Mika had thus retained the world title and Eddie, admittedly outraced decisively on this occasion, had missed out on probably his only real chance of the world title by two points. On the face of it, Schumacher was just as much a winner as Mika Häkkinen.

Think of it this way. Invalided out of seven Grands Prix with a broken leg, 'the Schu' sat back with mounting concern as Eddie launched his own bid for the championship. Some 20 years after Jody Scheckter last won a drivers' title at the wheel of a Ferrari, now Maranello's high-priced, much-touted multi-millionaire star was sitting in his Swiss villa watching his wingman heading towards championship glory. In Formula One terms, it was as though the corporate annual bonus stood poised to be dished out to the nightwatchman rather than the chairman of the board. Forget the fact that, in his own way, the nightwatchman had more charisma and charm than the chairman. It was a distinctly anomalous situation and one which Schumacher was obviously keen to redress.

He had two obvious options. One was to stay out for the entire year and concentrate on a full recovery for the 2000 season, keeping his fingers firmly crossed that Eddie would flunk the exercise without his assistance. The other was to make a return towards the end of the season and help Eddie's cause – while keeping his fingers crossed that this colleague would not make it.

Throughout this whole tortuous episode, one got the strong impression that Irvine had read the situation perfectly. In Malaysia, Michael had kept people guessing over just how much of a leg-up he was prepared to offer Eddie. For his part, Irvine clearly relished the situation in which Schumacher was making a return to the cockpit before the end of the season, ostensibly to offer a helping hand. However, he flatly refused to respond to speculation that the real reason Schumacher had changed his mind and decided to return before the end of the season was to demonstrate how things might have developed had he not been injured at Silverstone.

There were, of course, other views. 'Ferrari wants to make sure that, if it loses this year's World Championship, it will be portrayed as Eddie's fault,' said one source close to the Italian team. Could be, could be.

Come the race in Malaysia, Schumacher played the supporting role to perfection, twice handing the lead to Irvine. But that was as far as his benevolence extended. Going into the Japanese Grand Prix, he vowed that he was intending to win the race and everybody else could make their own arrangements. Schumacher's stated ambition was designed to show the spectating world how things might have turned out had he not been injured at Silverstone. In the event, however, Häkkinen took him apart.

Despite forensic evidence to the contrary hidden in the two cars' respective lap times, the author remains sceptical about the notion that Michael Schumacher threw the race. He might have settled for second, however, which is a very different thing altogether.

Irvine nevertheless viewed his season with satisfaction. He is one of the better-balanced members of the F1 community, with a reasonable perspective on his life. 'If in Melbourne you had told me that I would be second in the World Championship by just two points, I think I would have been happy settling for that,' he said in an observation which reflected no rancour or resentment.

One is bound to speculate how Irvine's prospects would have looked had the McLaren team opted to recruit him for the 2000 season as Mika Häkkinen's team-mate. Eventually, however, Britain's top F1 team took the conservative decision to stick with the eminently charming and promotable David Coulthard, some factions within McLaren perhaps feeling that Irvine's perceived firecracker temperament might be a bit too much for their sober management tone.

It could have been the wrong call. Irvine is far too clever not to tailor his behaviour to suit the prevailing environment in which he finds himself. He handled being Schumacher's team-mate with just the right blend of commitment and insouciance, despite remarking that 'driving as Michael's number two was like being hit round the head for four days at each Grand Prix.' Referring to his successor, Rubens Barrichello, who took over this difficult role at Ferrari, Irvine just remarked: 'God help him.'

For Irvine, the prospect of leading the rebranded Jaguar Racing team in 2000 offers him the role of number one in his own right. He may even win some more races. Nevertheless, one is bound to wonder whether the competitive stimulation of being figuratively beaten round the head for four days by Michael Schumacher is something he will eventually come to miss.

It certainly got the best out of him.

Appendix

Facts and figures

Starts	128
Championships	2
Race wins	35
Pole positions	23
Fastest laps	39
Points	570

Information correct at the beginning of the 2000 season

1991

Pos	Race	Circuit	Entrant	Car/engine	Comment	Grid
Ret	Belgium	Spa	Team 7UP Jordan	3.5 Jordan 191-Ford HB V8	Clutch	7
5	Italy	Monza	Camel Benetton Ford	3.5 Benetton B191-Ford HB V8		7
6	Portugal	Estoril	Camel Benetton Ford	3.5 Benetton B191-Ford HB V8		10
6	Spain	Barcelona	Camel Benetton Ford	3.5 Benetton B191-Ford HB V8		5
Ret	Japan	Suzuka	Camel Benetton Ford	3.5 Benetton B191-Ford HB V8	Engine	9
Ret	Australia	Adelaide	Camel Benetton Ford	3.5 Benetton B191-Ford HB V8	Collision	6

1992

Pos	Race	Circuit	Entrant	Car/engine	Comment	Grid
4	South Africa	Kyalami	Camel Benetton Ford	3.5 Benetton B191B-Ford HB V8		6
3	Mexico	Mexico City	Camel Benetton Ford	3.5 Benetton B191B-Ford HB V8		3
3	Brazil	Interlagos	Camel Benetton Ford	3.5 Benetton B191B-Ford HB V8	1 lap down	5
2	Spain	Barcelona	Camel Benetton Ford	3.5 Benetton B192-Ford HB V8		2
Ret	San Marino	Imola	Camel Benetton Ford	3.5 Benetton B192-Ford HB V8	Spin	5
4	Monaco	Monte Carlo	Camel Benetton Ford	3.5 Benetton B192-Ford HB V8		6
2	Canada	Montreal	Camel Benetton Ford	3.5 Benetton B192-Ford HB V8		5
Ret	France	Magny Cours	Camel Benetton Ford	3.5 Benetton B192-Ford HB V8	Accident	5
4	Great Britain	Silverstone	Camel Benetton Ford	3.5 Benetton B192-Ford HB V8		4
3	Germany	Hockenheim	Camel Benetton Ford	3.5 Benetton B192-Ford HB V8		7
Ret	Hungary	Hungaroring	Camel Benetton Ford	3.5 Benetton B192-Ford HB V8	Accident	4
1	Belgium	Spa	Camel Benetton Ford	3.5 Benetton B192-Ford HB V8		3
3	Italy	Monza	Camel Benetton Ford	3.5 Benetton B192-Ford HB V8	Clutch	6
7	Portugal	Estoril	Camel Benetton Ford	3.5 Benetton B192-Ford HB V8	2 laps down	5
Ret	Japan	Suzuka	Camel Benetton Ford	3.5 Benetton B192-Ford HB V8	Gearbox	5
2	Australia	Adelaide	Camel Benetton Ford	3.5 Benetton B192-Ford HB V8		5

1993

Pos	Race	Circuit	Entrant	Car/engine	Comment	Grid
Ret	South Africa	Kyalami	Camel Benetton Ford	3.5 Benetton B192B-Ford HB V8	Accident	3
3	Brazil	Interlagos	Camel Benetton Ford	3.5 Benetton B192B-Ford HB V8		4
Ret	Europe	Donington	Camel Benetton Ford	3.5 Benetton B193B-Ford HB V8		3
2	San Marino	Imola	Camel Benetton Ford	3.5 Benetton B193B-Ford HB V8		3
3	Spain	Barcelona	Camel Benetton Ford	3.5 Benetton B193B-Ford HB V8		4
Ret	Monaco	Monte Carlo	Camel Benetton Ford	3.5 Benetton B193B-Ford HB V8	Hydraulics	2
2	Canada	Montreal	Camel Benetton Ford	3.5 Benetton B193B-Ford HB V8		3
3	France	Magny Cours	Camel Benetton Ford	3.5 Benetton B193B-Ford HB V8		7
2	Great Britain	Silverstone	Camel Benetton Ford	3.5 Benetton B193B-Ford HB V8		3
2	Germany	Hockenheim	Camel Benetton Ford	3.5 Benetton B193B-Ford HB V8		3
Ret	Hungary	Hungaroring	Camel Benetton Ford	3.5 Benetton B193B-Ford HB V8	Fuel pump	3
2	Belgium	Spa	Camel Benetton Ford	3.5 Benetton B193B-Ford HB V8		3
Ret	Italy	Monza	Camel Benetton Ford	3.5 Benetton B193B-Ford HB V8	Engine	5
1	Portugal	Estoril	Camel Benetton Ford	3.5 Benetton B193B-Ford HB V8		6
Ret	Japan	Suzuka	Camel Benetton Ford	3.5 Benetton B193B-Ford HB V8	Accident	4
Ret	Australia	Adelaide	Camel Benetton Ford	3.5 Benetton B193B-Ford HB V8	Engine	4

1994 (World Champion)

Pos	Race	Circuit	Entrant	Car/engine	Comment	Grid
1	Brazil	Interlagos	Mild Seven Benetton Ford	3.5 Benetton B194-Ford Zetec-R V8		2
1	Pacific	T I Circuit	Mild Seven Benetton Ford	3.5 Benetton B194-Ford Zetec-R V8		2
1	San Marino	Imola	Mild Seven Benetton Ford	3.5 Benetton B194-Ford Zetec-R V8		2
1	Monaco	Monte Carlo	Mild Seven Benetton Ford	3.5 Benetton B194-Ford Zetec-R V8		1
2	Spain	Barcelona	Mild Seven Benetton Ford	3.5 Benetton B194-Ford Zetec-R V8		1
1	Canada	Montreal	Mild Seven Benetton Ford	3.5 Benetton B194-Ford Zetec-R V8		1
1	France	Magny Cours	Mild Seven Benetton Ford	3.5 Benetton B194-Ford Zetec-R V8		3
DSQ	Great Britain	Silverstone	Mild Seven Benetton Ford	3.5 Benetton B194-Ford Zetec-R V8	Black flag	2
Ret	Germany	Hockenheim	Mild Seven Benetton Ford	3.5 Benetton B194-Ford Zetec-R V8	Engine	4
1	Hungary	Hungaroring	Mild Seven Benetton Ford	3.5 Benetton B194-Ford Zetec-R V8		2
DSQ	Belgium	Spa	Mild Seven Benetton Ford	3.5 Benetton B194-Ford Zetec-R V8	Undertray wear	2
1	Europe	Jerez	Mild Seven Benetton Ford	3.5 Benetton B194-Ford Zetec-R V8		1
2	Japan	Suzuka	Mild Seven Benetton Ford	3.5 Benetton B194-Ford Zetec-R V8		1
Ret	Australia	Adelaide	Mild Seven Benetton Ford	3.5 Benetton B194-Ford Zetec-R V8	Collision	2

1995 (World Champion)

Pos	Race	Circuit	Entrant	Car/engine	Comment	Grid
1	Brazil	Interlagos	Mild Seven Benetton Ford	3.0 Benetton B195-Renault V10		2
3	Argentina	Buenos Aires	Mild Seven Benetton Ford	3.0 Benetton B195-Renault V10		3
Ret	San Marino	Imola	Mild Seven Benetton Ford	3.0 Benetton B195-Renault V10	Accident	1
1	Spain	Barcelona	Mild Seven Benetton Ford	3.0 Benetton B195-Renault V10		1
1	Monaco	Monte Carlo	Mild Seven Benetton Ford	3.0 Benetton B195-Renault V10		2
5	Canada	Montreal	Mild Seven Benetton Ford	3.0 Benetton B195-Renault V10	Gearbox	1
1	France	Magny Cours	Mild Seven Benetton Ford	3.0 Benetton B195-Renault V10		2
Ret	Great Britain	Silverstone	Mild Seven Benetton Ford	3.0 Benetton B195-Renault V10	Collision	1
1	Germany	Hockenheim	Mild Seven Benetton Ford	3.0 Benetton B195-Renault V10		2
11	Hungary	Hungaroring	Mild Seven Benetton Ford	3.0 Benetton B195-Renault V10	Fuel pump	3
1	Belgium	Spa	Mild Seven Benetton Ford	3.0 Benetton B195-Renault V10		16
Ret	Italy	Monza	Mild Seven Benetton Ford	3.0 Benetton B195-Renault V10	Collision	2
2	Portugal	Estoril	Mild Seven Benetton Ford	3.0 Benetton B195-Renault V10		3
1	Europe	Nürburgring	Mild Seven Benetton Ford	3.0 Benetton B195-Renault V10		3
1	Pacific	T I Circuit	Mild Seven Benetton Ford	3.0 Benetton B195-Renault V10		3
1	Japan	Suzuka	Mild Seven Benetton Ford	3.0 Benetton B195-Renault V10		1
Ret	Australia	Adelaide	Mild Seven Benetton Ford	3.0 Benetton B195-Renault V10	Collision	3

1996

Pos	Race	Circuit	No Entrant	Car/engine	Comment	Grid
Ret	Australia	Melbourne	Scuderia Ferrari	Ferrari 310 046 V10	Brakes	4
3	Brazil	Interlagos	Scuderia Ferrari	Ferrari 310 046 V10		4
Ret	Argentina	Buenos Aires	Scuderia Ferrari	Ferrari 310 046 V10	Rear wing	2
2	Europe	Nürburgring	Scuderia Ferrari	Ferrari 310 046 V10		3
2	San Marino	Imola	Scuderia Ferrari	Ferrari 310 046 V10		2
Ret	Monaco	Monte Carlo	Scuderia Ferrari	Ferrari 310 046 V10	Accident	1
1	Spain	Barcelona	Scuderia Ferrari	Ferrari 310 046 V10		3
Ret	Canada	Montreal	Scuderia Ferrari	Ferrari 310 046 V10	Driveshaft	3
DNS	France	Magny Cours	Scuderia Ferrari	Ferrari 310 046 V10	Engine	1
Ret	Great Britain	Silverstone	Scuderia Ferrari	Ferrari 310 046 V10	Hydraulics	3
4	Germany	Hockenheim	Scuderia Ferrari	Ferrari 310 046 V10		3
9	Hungary	Hungaroring	Scuderia Ferrari	Ferrari 310 046 V10	Throttle/7laps down	1
1	Belgium	Spa	Scuderia Ferrari	Ferrari 310 046 V10		3
1	Italy	Monza	Scuderia Ferrari	Ferrari 310 046 V10		3
3	Portugal	Estoril	Scuderia Ferrari	Ferrari 310 046 V10		4
2	Japan	Suzuka	Scuderia Ferrari	Ferrari 310 046 V10		3

1997

Pos	Race	Circuit	Entrant	Car/engine	Comment	Grid
2	Australia	Melbourne	Scuderia Ferrari Marlboro	Ferrari 310B 046 V10		3
5	Brazil	Interlagos	Scuderia Ferrari Marlboro	Ferrari 310B 046 V10		2
Ret	Argentina	Buenos Aires	Scuderia Ferrari Marlboro	Ferrari 310B 046 V10	Collision	4
2	San Marino	Imola	Scuderia Ferrari Marlboro	Ferrari 310B 046 V10		3
1	Monaco	Monte Carlo	Scuderia Ferrari Marlboro	Ferrari 310B 046 V10		2
4	Spain	Barcelona	Scuderia Ferrari Marlboro	Ferrari 310B 046 V10		7
1	Canada	Montreal	Scuderia Ferrari Marlboro	Ferrari 310B 046 V10		1
1	France	Magny Cours	Scuderia Ferrari Marlboro	Ferrari 310B 046/2 V10		1
Ret	Great Britain	Silverstone	Scuderia Ferrari Marlboro	Ferrari 310B 046/2 V10	Wheel bearing	4
2	Germany	Hockenheim	Scuderia Ferrari Marlboro	Ferrari 310B 046 V10		4
4	Hungary	Hungaroring	Scuderia Ferrari Marlboro	Ferrari 310B 046/2 V10		1
1	Belgium	Spa	Scuderia Ferrari Marlboro	Ferrari 310B 046/2 V10		3
6	Italy	Monza	Scuderia Ferrari Marlboro	Ferrari 310B 046/2 V10		9
6	Austria	A1-Ring	Scuderia Ferrari Marlboro	Ferrari 310B 046/2 V10		9
Ret	Luxembourg	Nürburgring	Scuderia Ferrari Marlboro	Ferrari 310B 046/2 V10	Accident	5
1	Japan	Suzuka	Scuderia Ferrari Marlboro	Ferrari 310B 046/2 V10		2
Ret	Europe	Jerez	Scuderia Ferrari Marlboro	Ferrari 310B 046/2 V10	Collision	2

1998

Pos	Race	Circuit	Entrant	Car/engine	Comment	Grid
Ret	Australia	Melbourne	Scuderia Ferrari Marlboro	Ferrari 300 047 V10	Engine	3
3	Brazil	Interlagos	Scuderia Ferrari Marlboro	Ferrari 300 047 V10		4
1	Argentina	Buenos Aires	Scuderia Ferrari Marlboro	Ferrari 300 047 V10		2
2	San Marino	Imola	Scuderia Ferrari Marlboro	Ferrari 300 047 V10		3
3	Spain	Barcelona	Scuderia Ferrari Marlboro	Ferrari 300 047 V10		3
10	Monaco	Monte Carlo	Scuderia Ferrari Marlboro	Ferrari 300 047 V10	2 laps down	4
1	Canada	Montreal	Scuderia Ferrari Marlboro	Ferrari 300 047 V10		3
1	France	Magny Cours	Scuderia Ferrari Marlboro	Ferrari 300 047 V10		2
1	Great Britain	Silverstone	Scuderia Ferrari Marlboro	Ferrari 300 047 V10		2
3	Austria	A1-Ring	Scuderia Ferrari Marlboro	Ferrari 300 047 V10		4
5	Germany	Hockenheim	Scuderia Ferrari Marlboro	Ferrari 300 047 V10		9
1	Hungary	Hungaroring	Scuderia Ferrari Marlboro	Ferrari 300 047 V10		3
Ret	Belgium	Spa	Scuderia Ferrari Marlboro	Ferrari 300 047 V10	Collision	4
1	Italy	Monza	Scuderia Ferrari Marlboro	Ferrari 300 047 V10		1
2	Luxembourg	Nürburgring	Scuderia Ferrari Marlboro	Ferrari 300 047 V10		1
Ret	Japan	Suzuka	Scuderia Ferrari Marlboro	Ferrari 300 047 V10	Puncture	1

1999

Pos	Race	Circuit	Entrant	Car/engine	Comment	Grid
8	Australia	Melbourne	Scuderia Ferrari Marlboro	Ferrari 399 048 V10	1 lap down	3
2	Brazil	Interlagos	Scuderia Ferrari Marlboro	Ferrari 399 048 V10		4
1	San Marino	Imola	Scuderia Ferrari Marlboro	Ferrari 399 048 V10		3
1	Monaco	Monte Carlo	Scuderia Ferrari Marlboro	Ferrari 399 048 V10		2
3	Spain	Barcelona	Scuderia Ferrari Marlboro	Ferrari 399 048 V10		4
Ret	Canada	Montreal	Scuderia Ferrari Marlboro	Ferrari 399 048 V10	Accident	1
5	France	Magny Cours	Scuderia Ferrari Marlboro	Ferrari 399 048 V10		6
DNS	Great Britain	Silverstone	Scuderia Ferrari Marlboro	Ferrari 399 048 V10	Accident	2
DNS six races						
2	Malaysia	Sepang	Scuderia Ferrari Marlboro	Ferrari 399 048B V10		1
2	Japan	Suzuka	Scuderia Ferrari Marlboro	Ferrari 399 048B V10		1

Q

Other motor sport books from Queensgate Publications

Track Record   Maurice Rowe   1-902655-00-1

The photography of *The Motor* magazine's former Chief Photographer, Maurice Rowe. Over 300 black and white and colour images from F1 and sports cars, 1950-1980.

Racers 1948-1968   Doug Nye   1-902655-01-X

Part One of two volumes celebrating the greatest drivers in F1. Doug Nye selects his Top 20, from Wimille to Hulme. Lavishly illustrated with over 250 photographs.

Racers 1969-2000   Alan Henry   1-902655-028

Part Two of the *Racers* series, celebrating the modern era of Grand Prix. *Autocar*'s long-time correspondent profiles his star drivers from Jochen Rindt to Mika Häkkinen.

Mika   Alan Henry   1-902655-26-5

Biography of the likeable Finnish driver who recovered from a horrific practice accident at the end of the 1995 season to win back-to-back world titles for McLaren–Mercedes.

The Grand Prix Bible   Mike Lawrence   1-902655-25-7

Encyclopaedic facts and figures guide to Formula 1. Driver histories, race facts, circuit details, technical information: this is the ultimate armchair guide.

Also from Queensgate Publications

Golf: A Mind Game   Butler/Galvin   1-902655-03-6

Action Guide Europe   Watkins/Grogan   1-902655-06-0

Queensgate is distributed in the UK by

MDL Sales
Macmillan Distribution Ltd
Brunel Road
Houndmills
Basingstoke
Hants RG21 6XS

Tel 01256 302775
Fax 01256 351437

Queensgate is distributed in the USA by

Trafalgar Square Publishing
PO Box 257
Howe Hill Road
North Pomfret
Vermont 05053

Tel 802 457 1911
Fax 802 457 1913
www.trafalgarsquarebooks.com